Is There a Man in the House?

Is There a Man in the House?

Carlton Pearson

Treasure House

An Imprint of
Destiny Image® Publishers, Inc.
P.O. Box 310
Shippensburg, PA 17257-0310

"For where your treasure is,
there will your heart be also." Matthew 6:21

ISBN 1-56043-270-5

Second Printing: 1999   Third Printing: 1999

For Worldwide Distribution
Printed in the U.S.A.

This book and all other Destiny Image, Revival Press,
and Treasure House books are available
at Christian bookstores and distributors worldwide

For a U.S. bookstore nearest you, call **1-800-722-6774**.
For more information on foreign distributors, call **717-532-3040**.
Or reach us on the Internet: **http://www.reapernet.com**

Dedication

This book is dedicated to my loving wife Gina and son Julian, without whose cooperation this project would not have been accomplished.

To my Mom and Dad, who made it possible for me to be a man in anybody's house!

To all the fathers who ever touched my life in my extended family and in ministry.

To Bishop J.A. Blake, Oral Roberts, and Dad Vaughn, whose love and friendship I cherish.

To Jesse Williams, Jr., Mike Williams, and my church staff, for their support and work on this project.

And last, but not least, to Higher Dimensions Family Church, who has allowed me the privilege of fathering them in the Spirit.

Contents

I looked for a man among them who would build up the wall and stand before Me in the gap on behalf of the land so I would not have to destroy it, but I found none (Ezekiel 22:30).

Preface

I began teaching on the subject "Is There a Man in the House" several years before I met my wife, Gina Marie. However, since I've been married, I've realized and can admit that I didn't really know the man in my house until I got the woman in my house. In other words, marriage can be a reflection of what you are and what you are not; what you should be and what you shouldn't.

Only two months into my marriage, my wife conceived, and nine months later, I was a father. While the marriage affirmed me as a man, fatherhood validated my masculinity and my manhood in a way my 40 years of prior living couldn't and didn't.

Throughout this book, I make repeated references to my wife and my son, Julian, not only because I love them and am so thrilled to have them in my life, but also because I am convinced that I could not adequately articulate on this subject without referring to the man who is a husband and a father (one who is learning by the grace of God to be accurate, exact, and more pronounced in that sacred function every day). It is through the relationship I have with my family, and the one I am developing with them daily, that I am discovering the man in my house.

My first example of a man in the house, I proudly admit, is my own dad, Adam Louis Pearson.

One of the most pronounced memories I have of growing up in the so-called ghettos of San Diego, California, is the morning our entire family was abruptly awakened before daylight by the alarming shrieks and screams of one of my sisters. She herself had been awakened by the heavy voice and weight of a man who had quietly slipped in through her bedroom window and was even then lying on top of her in the process of committing the brutal act of rape.

My dad had always said that he could never sleep soundly until he knew all his children were safely home and in bed with all the doors properly bolted shut and locked. Although we never told him so, I think it was the consensus of my mother and all of us children, that none of us could sleep securely or soundly until we knew he was there also. Even if the doors weren't properly locked, we knew Daddy could and would protect us from any unwanted intruders in our home.

The point was poignantly driven home to us the morning my sister's frantic screams caused everyone to suddenly jump out of their beds.

My brother and I shared a room, and our four sisters doubled up in two of the other bedrooms, with our parents in the so-called master bedroom. (It was actually one of two same-sized bedrooms we had added to our house when I was in the sixth grade.)

I don't know who heard the screams first; however, our bedroom was closest to the bedroom from where the screams were originating. My brother and I sat straight up in our beds and looked at each other with our mouths wide open in puzzled, panicked, and confused hesitancy. We weren't sure whether to run the opposite direction or go immediately toward the girls' bedroom.

We both admitted later that we were too scared to do anything at all but wait to take our cue from our dad. We were hoping he would get to our sisters' bedroom before we did.

My poor dad, still in a slight sleeping stupor, wasn't sure which direction the screams were coming from. He ran first to the girls' bedroom closest to his, and then to the one nearest us. I remember hearing him yell, "Where are you, babies?" to my screaming little sisters. We all yelled back, the two girls and my brother and I, "In here, Daddy, in here!" By the time my brother and I could get up the nerve to move (probably only a few seconds), my dad was already in my sister's bedroom. Through all the confusion, the intruder—who was later apprehended by the police and sent away to prison—had escaped through a window in the living room. As dad rushed into the room he kept asking, "What's wrong? What's wrong?" and the girls kept saying, "There was a man in here. There was a man in our house."

While we were all visibly shaken by the episode, I remember the solace, security, and sentimental pride I felt when I saw my dad standing there in his big, baggy boxer shorts holding and consoling the two baby girls and speaking calm and reassuring words of comfort to all of us. He seemed to have been saying, "It's all right. It's okay. You're all safe now." The intruder wasn't a real man; he was an unwelcome visitor, an impostor, a reproachable breach of manhood. My father's protective response indicated that he was the true man in our house. He was standing in the gap, making up the hedge of protection for our household. We all knew it. Mother knew it, the girls knew it, and my brother and I knew it.

In the verses preceding Ezekiel 22:30, our Lord seems to be defending Himself for the action He was about to take against Jerusalem. The city had become bloody, vile, and violent. The entire nation (Israel) had become dross. It had to be melted down by the judgment of God. All classes and all cultures of the people were guilty of ungodliness and sin. The Lord was looking for an intercessor, a priestly person, someone to stand before Him arbitrarily in repentant prayer and representative contrition, but He could find none.

The scenario in that passage sounds very much like America and our world today. The moral and social decay to which our nation has sunk is the blaring scandal of our times. As we come to the end of a decade, a century, and a millennium, God is calling for and calling up not just one man to stand in the gap and make up the hedge (wall of protection), but many men, all men—every race, color, and culture of men—to rise up to the divine cause and calling to put our houses and homes back in order. We'll do it by first aligning our own hearts, heads, and lives to the ordained purposes of God as outlined in the Scriptures, and then by following through with setting our homes, churches, schools, and yes, this entire nation, back in line with its original Judeo-Christian foundation, ethics, purposes, principles, and standards. Our work is cut out before us. The road is long and the distance seems far; however, our God has not forsaken us. His ultimate purposes for His people in America and on earth cannot and will not be ultimately thwarted.

The clarion call of the twenty-first century is, *Is There a Man in the House?* "Are you the man in your house? Can you be the man in your house? Will you be the man in your house?"

Foreword

Stabbing words are in the air today—but I'm not speaking of those flavored by hate or anger. Rather, it's the shake-awake, crisp and cutting call of the Holy Spirit, ripping through the ether like a band saw in a lumber mill: *Arise! Arise!*

God is calling men!

During the past few months, I've stood before multitudes of men in a dozen stadiums across America. Our nation's largest venues are becoming gathering sites for 50,000 to 80,000 men at a time, as this milestone miracle of a century-ending awakening among men throbs and pulsates forward. As we watch these stadia fill, we all know one thing for sure: *Only God could do this!* He's calling, waking, stirring, and drawing together *men!*

This book is of this spirit. It's a part of that "Voice" calling us to hear; it's of a distinct genre—a kind and quality of work that's tuned to and thundering that present-hour call that says to you and me, sir: "*There's more to this than 'hearing the call.' Having heard, we need to **answer it**!*"

Carlton Pearson's spirited and steadfast leadership has been stirring hearts for years, but it just might be that his greatest impact is on the verge of occurring. A confluence of factors seems to be surfacing his voice at a new dimension. Beyond and beside his solid pastoral service, proven at his Tulsa pastorate for more than 14 years and welcomed across the charismatic community throughout that time, something else is happening.

First, at an hour God is awakening men to *Christ's call,* Carlton stands tall with a prophetic anointing, pointing to the only way life really works—through God's Word and by His Spirit's power.

Second, at the very time God is dealing with men about *convictions,* Carlton is both speaking and writing to provide the kind of experienced and valuable insights that build steel into the substance of a man's soul.

Third, at this crucial moment when God is issuing an added mandate to *color*—"Reconcile and unite!"—Carlton already models long-term, vigorous leadership in this vital arena of God's love-in-action.

I can't encourage men more forcibly than what I feel right now: *Read and feed on "the right stuff."* Like astronauts being trained for a mission meant to break *from* the bonds of gravity, God's wanting to prep us for a break *out* of the bonds of our past. He wants to lift us from habits of irresponsibility and apathy that the world-spirit breeds in a man's soul, crippling him for effective leadership and emasculating his true potential for husbanding and fatherhood.

This book provides some of that kind of "stuff"—and it's written by a pastor-leader, a man and a husband, who's committed to helping good men rise to being better than ever.

Here's the "chow and the chart" for higher dimensions in life and relationships; for your living and your loving at deeper depths and unto higher heights.

Let's answer that call.

Pastor Jack Hayford
The Church On The Way
Van Nuys, California
March, 1996

Introduction

Fathers: The Endangered Species

We have become orphans and fatherless, our mothers like widows (Lamentations 5:3).

I was 40 years old before I became a father for the first time. It has been the most fascinating and promising opportunity and responsibility that life has afforded me up to this point. However, fathering and fatherhood are too different functions. The former involves only a few minutes of physical exercise, while the latter (true fatherhood) demands the involvement and participation of soul, spirit, and body.

As my dear friend, Dr. Edwin Louis Cole, often says, "Being male is a matter of birth, but being a man is a matter of choice. Any male can make babies, but it takes a man to be a real father."

About 36 percent of America's children will sleep tonight in homes where their dads no longer live. In 1994 alone, there were 1.2 million divorces, about 53 percent of which involved minor children (according to the February 27, 1995, issue of *U.S. News and World Report*).

Mankind in general becomes more selfish and morally corrupt with each passing day. If you doubt it, just watch the evening news for a week. There are more horror stories in the news than Hollywood can make into films! The world is losing hope in the face of global mass destruction.

Satan has launched an all-out attack against the male seed. It is an attack against the headship of the family...an unholy assault against fathers, against husbands, and against the future generation! Some of the results of those attacks are these:

1. Men are dying early deaths from stress and from terminal diseases related to stress and to environmental causes.

2. The life expectancy of males is seven years less than females.

3. Three out of every four suicide victims in this country are men!

4. I am told that three out of four retarded children are little boys.

5. Men are 25 times more likely to be committed to a mental hospital than women.

6. Men have higher crime rates in all areas. They commit 90 percent of all violent crimes, and nearly 100 percent of all rapes. Ninety-four percent of all drunk driving accidents are caused by men, and they have a 365 percent higher arrest rate than women! Ninety to ninety-five percent of the reported crimes of incest are perpetrated by men.

How can you be a man among men and a righteous father if you did not have that model lived out in front of you?

How can you trust God as Father, if you could not trust your own father to be a good parent?

Today, on the downhill side of this decade, this century, and this millennium, many women are opposed to staying at home and attending primarily to the home and family. The economy has been affected so much by society's move away from God that, for America, prosperity seems on its way out. It takes two salaries for almost every family to make it, and most mothers have to work. This trend started as far back as the "Roaring Twenties." But the more women began to become breadwinners, however, the more men felt free to leave home if and when they wanted to.

As a result of the conspicuous absence of men from the home, many women are even developing the attitude that fathers are unnecessary. Some are even saying that they believe the family can do just fine without a man in the house. They are willing to take on the responsibility of a child without the "baggage" of a man. Unfortunately, they are transferring that same attitude to their children.

Fatherhood in the traditional sense is becoming a thing of the past, particularly in this country. Motherhood by nature still exists, although the "right to choose" whether your unborn baby lives or dies is no longer God's or the father's but the mother's in many countries.

Out-of-wedlock births, desertion, divorce, incarceration, and homosexuality are fast depleting the ranks of male leadership in the family. It seems that fathers in America ought to be added to "the endangered species list"!

Something is seriously wrong with the souls and spirits of the male members of the human race, which has brought America to the brink of a crisis. If we are going to restore spiritual order in our families and our nation, then we first need to have a clear picture of what that order is and what standards we are using to measure it.

What elements in our culture and society has the devil been able to use to cause this crisis?

The first thing he did was to foment world wars in this century in which death gobbled up a large percentage of American men who were strong, honorable, and God-fearing. Those were the men who made good husbands and fathers as well as the best patriotic male citizens. Those were the men who would fight the hardest, "hang in" dangerous situations the longest, and give their lives for those they loved.

The Roaring Twenties saw the first results of world war on American society. The war itself took thousands of men out of their homes, leaving the wives and mothers to fend for themselves. Women then became restless, bored, and even suspicious of their husbands. Eventually they began to want the same freedom to sin as men! Bootleg liquor, short skirts (ten years earlier it was a shame for a woman to show her ankle), and women moving out of the home into the workplace really began in the 1920's.

I certainly do not think women ought to go back to pinning their hair in a bun, dragging their skirts on the ground, and staying at home as in the 20's. However, my point is that to get us to the licentious, ungodly, perverted society of today, the devil used seemingly harmless, even sometimes good, small beginnings. A seed of rebellion coated in the sugar of freedom from oppression and the scent of prosperity has resulted in a deadly harvest of poisonous plants.

The problem is that when you give satan an inch, he takes a mile.

By the time the surviving servicemen of this country came home from World War II, their women had somehow been bitten and smitten by satan's venomous poison of independence and self-promotion. Wartime jobs gave women the incentive to move full-time into the marketplace. Working at a job or career, however, is not the problem.

What satan did was to subtly make working outside the home *more* desirable than being a wife and mother, which is still the highest responsibility and career God has given to women.

Also, many of today's men grew up in those years without a father to give headship, to approve them as they grew to manhood, and to be a role model. This present generation, children of the Baby Boomers from World War II, is like a flock of sheep without a shepherd or a group of blind men trying to lead one another around.

Statistics show that 57 percent of the men in prison grew up without both parents in the home. Studies also show that an absentee father is a better indicator of whether a man will become a criminal than either his race or economic status.

Men have a 31 percent higher marital impediment rate than women. Christian counselors say that up until about a decade ago, the majority of their practice involving sexual problems in marriage were men wanting help because wives were not meeting their needs. Today, they say, it is about 50-50. How can a man be a man in bed if he is not one in the living room, the kitchen, or in the workplace?

The problems men face are massive, multiple, and accumulative. In short, men have been affected in more severe ways by satanic onslaughts than women. Men, we need to reverse the trend of these mortal liabilities and begin to live according to the design of our Creator!

Many men are agitated and alarmed at such increasingly widespread problems with manhood, marriage, and the family. It has caused them to take a long and probing look at themselves. Most are now ready, willing, and eager to change, repent, or even reform in order to fulfill their God-ordained responsibilities...at least in the Christian world.

It is difficult to face these issues, but until we address them openly and confront them directly, the enemy will continue to undermine human society. We need to call sin by its name and launch a counterattack against the enemy! In today's liberal climate, the topic of masculine leadership of the family is becoming an unpopular subject.

The so-called "new maleness" incorporates the performance of domestic chores and duties in the home formerly attributed primarily to females, which in some instances is a good thing. If both husband and wife have to work at jobs, then both should share the home chores. However, where do we draw the line?

Is there a difference between fairness in the home and the development of a "unisex" generation? If so, what is the difference? The next generation seems well on the way to men and women looking alike and acting alike. We seem to be headed toward the general blending of the genders, called androgyny.

That is the bad news! Now for the good: I believe the best for marriage and the family is yet to come.

As a full-time minister, one of my greatest challenges is to help enhance to maturity male Christians, teaching them how to be godly husbands, fathers, and leaders. This book covers topics such as:

- How to be meek without appearing weak.

- How to exert strength and forceful leadership without appearing mean, arrogant, and tyrannical.
- How to become godly leaders, servants, and models.

Studies by the National Bureau of Economic Research report that when an urban black man attends church, he is less likely to follow a life of crime. Church attendance is a more important factor than whether he comes from a home dependent on welfare, whether his parents are divorced, or whether he grows up in a public housing project.

Carl Wilson, founder of the Worldwide Discipleship Foundation, has said:

> "The family, with the traditional, Biblical roles for men and women in lifelong monogamous, marriage relationships, is the abiding natural foundation for social order, happiness, and stability. When that view is abandoned for selfish individualism, the society will collapse and die, the initiating cause being man's distorting his role which then initiates family decline. Therefore, the renewal of society must begin with men."[1]

Ultimately, the only answer to the problem of satan's attack on the male seed is the pattern set by Jesus Christ. By following His example as the perfection of mankind, we can have victory over all the schemes of the devil. We need to rise up and take our rightful place in our families, our churches, and in the Body of Christ at large. Our nation's survival depends upon our doing exactly that! By the help and hand of God, we will!

We must answer one critical question: *Is There a Man in the House?*

Chapter 1

A Land of Widows

*There is a conspiracy of her princes within her like a roaring lion tearing its prey; they devour people, take treasures and precious things and **make many widows** within her* (Ezekiel 22:25).

America has become a land where a growing number of bereaved and bitter women are struggling to "make do" without breadwinners, protectors, or fathers for their children.

It reminds me of the time when Goliath, a nine-foot giant, held all of Israel's soldiers at bay for days. This one man held an entire army, including King Saul, in fear and trembling (see 1 Sam. 17).

At that point they were fighting like the medieval stories of King Arthur and his knights: rather than the entire army engaging in masive combat, they would select the largest and strongest individual soldier in each army to fight one-on-one.

Who would fight on the Lord's side? A young, untried shepherd boy said he and the Lord were a majority. He and the Lord could defeat any giant at any time! So David with only a slingshot and five smooth stones faced Goliath with his heavy armor, shield, and sword—and took him out with one shot (see 1 Sam. 17:40,49-50).

Once again, a godless Goliath (the present post-Christian, humanistic, secular culture) has captured the ears of millions of impotent males. He loudly boasts of their inability to provide for and protect their own. The combination of his threats, their guilt, and the anger of their women has emasculated many men in this country. America essentially has become a land of "widows."

"I looked for a man...but I found none" (Ezek. 22:30). As our society hemorrhages to death from self-inflicted wounds, there is a conspicuous lack of strong, responsible, and decisive male leadership. We need a "David," a cadre of Christian men who will say, "Who is this uncircumcised Philistine?" It won't take a huge army to defeat the present Goliath; only a core of dedicated, sanctified, and courageous Christian men.

The spirit of murder has been unleashed in our land. Its goals are to destroy our children before they are born, to destroy the manhood of our living males, and to separate husbands from the households they are ordained to bind together.

Present in Body Only

Half the marriages in America fail in bitter divorce or outright abandonment by the husbands, and many husbands who are still in the home are "present in body only." They are spiritually dead and impotent, walking pretenders whose brains have shut down, whose hearts have lost the very passion of life! They are unable or unwilling to accept the responsibility of being a man in their homes.

For too much of the time, the American male is dead at home, dead in the bedroom, and dead on the job!

Millions of women are in mourning over "what might have been...." They have bitterly buried their unfulfilled dreams of a good marriage, along with every hope of receiving the love, honor, and respect they thought would come with the marriage vows. Our nation is reeling under the anguished cries of a rising flood of angry and broken women whose husbands and dreams have been stolen or killed by satan's devices!

God is searching the land for men, for husbands and fathers, who will dare to stand up in the face of open opposition and say, "Who is trying to take over my family, my wife, and my nation? Who does he think he is? He will have to go through me first—let me at him!"

The Church has endured satan's taunts and bullying for many years. Although there are many males in this country and in the Church, most of them have not been willing to stand up and be counted for right. For years, the congregations of most churches have been predominantly female.

God is looking for *men who will dare to do something*! As long as America's males continue to cave in to selfish desires and the devil's threats, this nation will continue its rapid downward slide to destruction and spiritual captivity.

The Bible and human history show us that, when satan cannot kill the leaders in a generation, he will devise a way to kill the children before they have a chance to grow into leaders. He does this because he has learned that God launches every earthshaking movement to save His people through the birth of a little child of destiny!

This Is Nothing New!

It all started with Adam and Eve. Eve was the first woman, wife, and mother to experience the bitter fruit of the thief's work. She lost her intimate relationship with God, she lost her loving relationship with her husband, and she ultimately lost her two oldest sons because of the devil's determination to destroy Adam's seed and avoid God's curse over his head (see Gen. 3:14-15).

The quickest way to kill a person is to strike at the head. That is also the quickest way to kill or disable marriages, families, armies, nations, and churches! An equally effective but slower method is to eliminate the means of reproduction and nurturing by striking at the female, the home, and the child. The disintegration of the American family perfectly illustrates this devilish strategy and its effectiveness!

Satan is out to strike at the head of the family and the leaders of our nation by killing or figuratively emasculating men. He has also demeaned the value and distorted the vital roles of women ever since he deceived and robbed Eve in the garden. Finally, he is striking at our seed with the vicious double-bladed axe of abortion and the removal of true men and genuine manhood from the homes of America and the world.

Satan Attacks the Head

> *Submit to one another out of reverence for Christ. Wives, submit to your husbands as to the Lord. For the husband is the head of the wife as Christ is the head of the church, His body, of which He is the Savior* (Ephesians 5:21-23).

The Bible says the husband is the "head of the wife." According to *Strong's Comprehensive Concordance to the Bible*, the

Greek word for "head" used in Ephesians is *kaphale,* a derivative of the Greek word *kapto.* This is where we get the English words *capita, capital,* and *captain* or *chieftain.* It means "head, both of men and, often, of animals."

Since the loss of the head destroys life, this word is used in phrases relating to capital or extreme punishment (capital punishment in America suggests death through execution). It is a metaphor for anything "supreme, chief, prominent; of persons, master, lord: or of a husband in relation to his wife; or of Christ in relation to the Church."[2]

Across this nation and throughout the Church, husbands have abandoned their wives and run from their responsibilities because of satan's aggressive attack!

The head is the seat or primary source of vision, and is the site of speech, thought, and most of the bodily senses. Your body can survive and adapt after the amputation of a leg or an arm. In our day, life can even be sustained after the transplant of a lung, a kidney, or even a heart—but you cannot transplant or amputate a head.

God gives grace to families, churches, and nations who suffer the loss of husbands and male leaders, but these situations represent disruptions of God's original plan. Understand that man's assignment as the head is a matter of *function,* not of value or superior worth.

Without the head, there is no vision. Where there is no vision, the people perish, for they will cast off restraint and lose all discipline (Prov. 29:18, paraphrased). Does that have a familiar ring to it?

How would you define our society each night after watching the national and local news?

Now you know why the devil is "decapitating" our families, our society, and the Church! We have headless leadership, and anything without a head is a monster. Anything with more than one head is considered a freak. Terror is spreading across the land for the same reason terror struck the fictitious town of Sleepy Hollow in Washington Irving's famous tale, "The Headless Horseman Rides Again," which some TV networks always run each year about the time of Halloween. There's something ugly and frightening about a headless body.

America and families worldwide are yearning for headship! We all want a fathering spirit in our lives. Everyone needs a dad. We are crying, "Abba, Father!" We need responsible, God-ordained heads and headship.

Throughout history, satan has attempted to destroy God's servants and replace His designated "heads" on earth with himself. He usurped Adam's authority through deception in the garden. He even tried to "transplant" the Head of the Church—Jesus Christ—through beguilement. During the temptation in the wilderness, he asked Jesus to worship him in return for all the nations of the earth (see Mt. 4:8-10). When satan's attempted "transplant" did not succeed, he thought he could avoid the curse in Genesis by killing our Savior, but he couldn't. Jesus laid down His own life as a sacrifice for our sins and rose victorious from the grave to sit at the right hand of the Father.

The Destiny of the Male Seed

So the Lord God said to the serpent, "Because you have done this, Cursed are you.... And I will put enmity between you and the woman, and between your offspring and hers; he will crush your head, and you will strike his heel" (Genesis 3:14-15).

The Bible says that the seed of woman (meaning the male seed), would bruise or crush the head of the serpent (satan). The Hebrew word translated as "bruise" is *shuwph*. It means "to gape, snap at, or overwhelm."[3]

God prophesied that the male seed—ultimately Jesus Christ—would crush or snap off the devil's head! Mankind—through the one Man, Jesus Christ—would take the devil (the serpent) by the tail and literally snap his head off. Satan was destined, cursed, and designated by God to be deposed, defeated, defanged, and decapitated!

I also discovered that "head" sometimes refers to "rank or rule." Through Jesus Christ, satan has been demoted and stripped of his rank. It is the calling and anointing of God-fearing, Spirit-led men to keep him underfoot. We outclass and outrank him through the life and blood of Jesus.

The earthly role, responsibility, and authority of the male in the Body of Christ is to crush the devil's head! That is the part of man's responsibility as head, shield, and protector in the marriage, the family, and the Church.

God never called a woman to crush the devil's head, although she has direct access to the name and power of Jesus Christ, along with all the armor and weapons of God. God laid that responsibility on the shoulders of men, and *He called women to do what no man could ever do*—birth the male seed that would crush the enemy's head. Women also bear the female seed that gives birth to and nurtures later generations of righteous male and female seed.

The Terminator Is Home

When a real man comes on the scene, the devil runs from him. The Bible says that all the serpent will do is bruise man's heel. The heel brings up the rear, and though it is important, it is not as vital as the head or the heart. The heel may sting with pain after a blow from satan, but our enemy was terminally damaged by Jesus when He hung on the cross at Calvary. Jesus just grabbed the serpent and popped his head off at the cross.

When men really step into their places in Christ, they are both literally and figuratively stepping on the devil's head. They are "bruising the head of the serpent" (see Gen. 3:15). They have a commission to be God's holy "terminators," with all authority to search out and destroy the works of the enemy. We just reach down, grab satan, and snap his head off! Our daily walk with Christ in the spirit is a daily routing out of satanic schemes and operatives. We are divinely authorized to "tread on serpents and scorpions" (Lk 10:19 KJV).

Isaiah 9:6a (KJV) declares, "For unto us a child is born, unto us a son is given" (speaking of Jesus).

What is the significance of that verse? Jesus is the gift of God, the Son who was commissioned to carry on the legacy of God's love in the earth.

All children born on this earth are precious and beautiful, but sons are given or gifted to us with a special spiritual significance related to their leadership function. (Daughters have an equally unique and precious spiritual significance, as you will see later.)

Satan knows that he was sentenced to be crushed by the heel of the male seed. He has known about his destiny and man's destiny since the fall, and he wants to put a stop to the destiny of the male seed before it even begins. This is why the devil takes such pleasure in killing babies—literal human babies, as well as baby dreams and ideas, baby visions, baby ministries, young churches, young marriages, and young people. If you have not noticed, there is a real war going on here.

Babies represent not only a threat to satan, but a promise to the saints!

There is a strong possibility that many of the 20 million babies aborted in the past 20 years in this country were males. Janis Sharpe, wife of Pastor Brent Sharpe, head of counseling in my church, Higher Dimensions in Tulsa, Oklahoma, counsels women who have had abortions. For years, she has asked these women to pray and ask God to show them what kind of child they aborted. These women then name the child they never brought to term, so the child has significance in their own lives; and they can have proper closure and forgiveness of the treacherous act of abortion.

According to Janis, 90 percent of the women who go through this process say they felt a strong impression that they had aborted a male child! Even if only half of the babies murdered through abortions every year are male, then the devil is successfully killing a large portion of the male seed before it ever gets planted in the earth!

Eve's name literally means "life-giver," but the devil has made modern-day Eves into life-takers! That is the murderous spirit of abortion at work. *When men began to abort their roles, women began to abort their babies!*

When a man functions in his proper role, the woman in his life is usually anxious to bring forth his baby. She is glad to provide and produce fruit for the man she loves and on whom she depends. When men run from the responsibilities of the marriage covenant and of headship, they are out of joint, out of balance, and out of place.

A pastor friend of mine, Brian K. Williams, often says, "The man out of his place makes the woman displaced, the children misplaced, and God ultimately replaced" (by drugs, alcohol, money, careers, etc.).

Women are frustrated because men are standing idly by and letting them confront the satanic onslaught alone—exactly as Adam did to Eve centuries ago! Women in general can never ultimately fufill their purpose until men fulfill theirs.

Satan was able to get to Eve because Adam was not functioning in his place as protector and shield. Adam watched his wife have a satanic encounter and did nothing about it. The truth today is the same as it was in the beginning: The devil cannot get to a woman if a man assumes his rightful place.

Abuse Is Abnormal Use

The Christian faith is built squarely upon the doctrine of reconciliation. God reconciled the world to Himself when Jesus went to the cross. At His ascension, He turned over to us both the message and the ministry of reconciliation (see Mt. 28:18-20; Mk. 16:15-18; Lk. 24:46-49; Acts 1:8; 2 Cor. 5:18-20).

Men must begin the reconciliation process in their own families before they take on the world. There are business professionals out there making fantastic business deals as well as ministers out preaching the gospel whose families are falling apart because of neglect and abuse! What have we gained if we lose our own wives and children? That loss can practically nullify anything else we've accomplished, not to mention the damage it does to our Christian testimony. *It is time we pull the splinter out of our own eyes before we try to pull a board out of our brother's* (see Lk. 6:42).

God requires men to manage their families, but He never gave them a license to be overbearing dictators! Many men abuse their wives physically, mentally, verbally, and spiritually, while claiming they are "bringing her into submission." A woman will never submit in her heart to a man who uses his fists on her face! She may do his bidding, but only to survive. Thus he destroys any love she ever had for him.

My friend Myles Munroe, in addressing the subject of purpose, shows that the word *abuse* comes from two English words meaning "abnormal use." You abnormally use a thing when you do not know its purpose. If you don't know the purpose of a knife and use it to hammer nails, you will damage it. So it is with anything else used improperly—it is always demeaning and ultimately destructive.

Many men abuse their wives because they do not know the divine purpose of a woman. Women can abuse their husbands for the same reason: They do not know God's purpose for the man.

Show Respect to Earn Respect

Any husband who continually shows disrespect for his wife will see his children disrespect her too. Any wife who constantly complains about her husband and runs him down in front of their children will notice the children begin to view their father with contempt. If parents mistreat their children or show favoritism, the children will do the same to one another.

Husband, when your wife is attacked by satan, step in as the representative of Jesus and say, "Devil, leave my woman alone!" That is a primary function of *agape* love.

The first time I saw my wife go through a major satanic attack (fear, anxiety, hysteria, etc.), I didn't recognize what was happening. I found myself agitated and defensive rather than supportive and prayerful. I felt threatened and out of control. I wanted to fix her and fix everything else, but I was reacting in fear (alarm) rather than responding in faith. It is during those times of stress and confrontation that godly men must love their wives more than they love themselves (see Phil. 2:3-4).

Paul says, "Husbands, love your wives..." (Eph. 5:25). That is a protective, enhancing, embracing, caressing love. Any woman would submit to a man like that.

America, the land of the widows and the home of the abandoned child, is in desperate need of real men of God who will stand in the gap! God is searching the land and scouring the churches for godly men who will challenge the thief to his face and demand that he return the stolen goods! The key to understanding how we got into this crisis is found where it all began—in the Garden of Eden.

Chapter 2

When God Said, "It Is Not Good"

The Lord God said, "It is not good for the man to be alone.
I will make a helper suitable for him" (Genesis 2:18).

I was 40 years old when I met and married my wife. There had been many opportunities to marry in earlier years—women who were nice, beautiful, talented, and devout Christians. However, I had determined not to marry until God said, "This is the one I have chosen for you." I learned a long time ago that whatever God chooses suits me better than anything I can choose for myself.

Can you imagine what it was like in today's culture being single for 40 years with all the thoughts, and sometimes fears, not to mention the questions, that came to mind? I had questions about manhood, mankind, manliness, "man-moods," *ad infinitum*. During those years, I began to study why God created us male and female.

In the beginning, God created—everything.

Each time He created something, whether it was the earth, the heavens, or the man He formed from the earth,

He declared before all creation, "It is good" (see Gen. 1:10,18,31). Our race was pure and holy (in the image of God in nature and character) in the beginning, and our roles and purposes for existence were clear and exact (see Gen. 1:26-28).

The Hebrew term for "good" is actually interpreted as "best," or "complete," or in a figurative sense, as "final or conclusive." The one and only time God said it was not good (conclusive) was when He referred to Adam as being alone.

As I began to study the origin of man and his original purpose, I discovered some fascinating insights and some very resourceful and even consoling, as well as explanatory, tidbits of information.

According to Genesis 2:18, God said, "...It is not good for the man to be alone...." Moffatt's translation does not use the article "the" in front of man. It just says "it is not good for man [*adom*, meaning mankind] to be alone."

The Hebrew word for "alone," I discovered, is *bad* (I am not kidding). According to *Strong's Concordance, bad* means "only, solitary, separate or separated."[4] In other words, God had created every other creature with both the male and female genders, but for mankind at that point, He only had the male. God simply was saying that man was not yet "good," or complete. He was not finished with His original intentions for man, which included forming the female out of the male in order for their union to facilitate procreation.

Four Ways of Describing Man

The Bible uses four different Hebrew words to refer to man: *adom, ish, zakar,* and *enosh.*

    1. *Adom* or Adam (from *adamah*, "earth") was God's first word for man. According to *Strong's*, it means

"red, ruddy, rosy, to be flushed (show blood in face)."[5] Figuratively, it means to be taken out of the red earth, as in clay. Human beings show blood in the face. *Adom* refers to "humankind," to human beings who breathe and think.

2. The second term for man is *ish*. It means "manly, robust, male person, husband," and so forth.[6] When God said, "I looked for a man" in Ezekiel 22:30, He used the word *ish*. It means a manly, robust male person or human.

3. The third word used in Hebrew for man is *zakar*. It means "to remember, mark, distinguish, designate, specially design (decorate)."[7] God distinguished, designated, and especially designed the male so he would not be overlooked. Even in the animal kingdom, the male species is always more decorative, particularly in the bird world. The plumage of the male bird is distinctively more colorful than the plumage of the female bird.

God marked the male for a reason, and the devil knows it.

No, the male is not "better" than the female, for God made them very similar anatomically and biologically, and it takes both "halves" to make a whole. He marked or "designated" both sexes, but in different ways. The female man was given an internal or hidden marking when she was created with a womb. Thus she is "the womb-man" or "the man with the womb."

God externally distinguished or "decorated" males, and it is around that "decoration" that He cut the blood covenant with Abraham centuries later (see

Gen. 15,17). This became the supreme type and shadow of the spiritual reality that would come with the death and resurrection of the Messiah, when spiritual circumcision would mark our exclusive separation unto God.

4. The fourth Hebrew word for man is *enosh*. It means "mortal, dust, dirt, death. To be frail, feeble, weak, incurable, terminal."[8] It refers to fallen man—the unregenerate human race. In other words, *enosh* is a man destined to die.

Psalm 8:4 says, "What is man [*enosh*] that You are mindful of him, the son of man that You care for him?"

Mankind is still asking that same question: "What is mortal, dying, incurable, terminally-ill mankind that You are mindful of him, God?"

The only answers to our dilemma are found in the Word of God. Mankind will only continue on its destructive path and drag civilization with it until we learn who we are in Christ. Confusion over purpose will continue until we learn we are the children of the living God, destined and designed to emulate Him in character, spirit, and purpose on earth.

The "Adom" With the Womb

After I met Gina, fell in love with her, and we decided to marry, I became as interested in the womb-man as I had been in the male man. Where did she come from? Why was she sent (made), and what was God's original purpose for her?

I knew that if I could learn these things, marriage would be much less of the traumatic surprise it is to most couples. Let's look at the first chapter of the Book of Genesis:

*Then God said, "Let Us make man [**adom**—mankind] in Our image, in Our likeness, and let **them** rule...." So God created man in His own image, in the image of God He created him; male and female He created them* (Genesis 1:26-27).

The first term God used for woman was the same word He used for man, for in the very beginning, both were one in the body of Adam. The Scriptures are clear: God had woman in mind from the very beginning. He said, "Let Us make man [*adom*] in Our image...and let *them* rule..." (Gen. 1:26).

The word *adom* referred to both the masculine and feminine embodied in the first human being. The woman is a female man. The male came first, but that does not make the female inferior or second-best. Secondary is not synonymous with "second best." Together, as one, man and woman were empowered to rule over every living creature.

The second Hebrew word applied to the woman later named Eve was translated as "female." It first appears in Genesis 1:27: "...in the image of God He created him; male and female He created them."

This Hebrew word translated as "female" is *n'qaba*, or *naqab*. The root word means "to puncture, literally (to perforate, with more or less violence), or figuratively (to specify, designate as distinct from the male...)." Additional meanings include "appoint, bore, name, pierce, strike through."[9]

The third term applied to Eve was *isshah*, or wife, the feminine of *ish* (man). Thus a female is a feminine male, a softer, more pliable male or man.

Every major aspect of a woman's body is specifically geared toward childbearing and the nurturing of children.

God marked or "designated" woman by making a cavity (womb) in her body for the baby before birth and by equipping her with mammary glands with which to nourish children. These two identifying characteristics are named in Jacob's blessing over his long-lost son, Joseph, in Genesis 49:25.

The primary Hebrew terms for "womb" are *rechem* and *recham*. They mean "to fondle; by implication, to love compassionately, as in cherishing the fetus in the womb."[10] In the New Testament, the main Greek word translated as "womb," *koilia*, is also translated as "belly," as in the verse that says, "Out of his belly shall flow rivers of living water" (Jn. 7:38b KJV).

Most men do not understand the delicacy of "the man with the womb." The woman is both delicate and strong. A woman is special because God has designed her for procreation. She bears and nurtures young. The first woman most men ever love is their mother. She carries him in her womb for nine months and is the first to bond with him, although as we have seen, more and more mothers are not fulfilling the mother function.

Before the days of bottled and canned baby formula, every baby boy took his first meals at his mother's breasts, usually at least for the first year. Many women have been returning to the practice of breast-feeding as medical science continues to find important reasons proving its nutritional, emotional, and medical importance to young infants.

During the nine months when a woman goes through the creative process of bringing forth a child, her husband can only stand by and watch. If he is honest, he will tell you it makes him feel useless, or at least less significant than before.

Once the baby is born, the child still needs the mother more than the father for months, but it is all part of God's plan.

As a father, I have tried to be as involved and participate as strongly in the nurturing process as possible. Yet there is only so much a father can do. He is no match for a full-time mother. I was amazed at my wife when our little boy, Julian, was born. Being a mother did not seem new to her. It seemed as if she had been a mother forever.

I have noticed that she never stops the nurturing process. She continues to feed and nurture our son as he grows through different stages. She nursed him as needed around the clock, changed his diapers, and bathed him. When he is teething and feverish (as he was at this writing), she picks him up and holds him. She carries and rocks him, and she sings him to sleep. When he cries in the night, Mother Gina is there. I often attend to him when he awakens in the night, but it's nothing like when his mother does.

As men witness the miracle of birth and see this little newcomer monopolize the majority of their wives' time and attention, which previously was spent with them, many men feel a little of what Eve might have felt in the Garden of Eden. Perhaps Eve was jealous of the time God spent with Adam.

You can almost hear her say, "Why was he here first? Why does he have such intimacy with God? When every other creature came from the dust, why am I the only one who came from Adam?" In the same manner many men often lament, "Why can't my wife be as accessible, accommodating, caring, and tolerant of me as she is of our little infant?"

The Incubator and Helper

Adam first referred to his wife as Eve in Genesis 3:20: "Adam named his wife Eve, because she would become the mother of all the living." The English name "Eve" comes from *Eva*, a Latin transliteration of *Chavvah*, the original Hebrew word in the text that means "life-giver."[11] The male is the cultivator; the female is the incubator. Eve is the mother of all living humans.

Adam did not give his wife an individual name until after all the other names in creation had been issued. First he called her "wife," *isshah* (see Gen. 2:24). Only after their expulsion from the garden did Adam call her Eve.

Remember, she was wife before she was mother, and that is still God's ideal for marriage. Once the babies begin to arrive, women tend to emphasize motherhood over wifehood in a disproportionate way. Most feel the children need them more than their husbands do, and they tend to put husbands on "the back burner" until children are in school. That is a mistake that usually causes significant regret later on in the family. A wife must always be a wife first and foremost. That sacred trust must remain the priority throughout the life of the marriage. Men need this, but are often afraid or at least hesitant to say so.

In ancient Israel, God instructed that a man should take off work and lay aside other duties for the first year of his marriage to "cheer up" his wife (see Deut. 24:5). If a man and a woman spend at least the first year getting to know one another intimately before beginning a baby, they would be more ready to welcome children into their union.

Women do not create seed; they incubate seed in a fertilized egg. Only females are designed to receive and incubate seed until it becomes another living human being. But even today, every woman must be careful about the "seed" she incubates. The "serpent's seed" will always yield a harvest of rebellion, destruction, and death.

A woman also is "one called alongside a man to help." The Greek translation of the Old Testament, the Septuagint, calls woman a *parakletos,* or in English, *paraclete.* It means "comforter or helper." This is the same word Jesus used in John 16:7 to describe the work of the Holy Spirit!

Eve was created as Adam's "helpmeet." Its Hebrew root, *ezer* or *azar,* means "to surround, to protect, to aid, or to give succor."[12] Man does not receive aid and comfort from work; he is to receive it from his wife.

As many ministers declare in marriage ceremonies, "The woman did not come from man's head to be over him, nor from his feet to be under him, but she came from his side to be near him and to help him."

God made man in His image, but He said that Adam needed someone outside of himself to surround him with love. He needed someone to pray for him and to nurture the seeds of his dreams. He needed a paraclete, a helpmeet to come to his aid.

The Home-Bonder (Husbandry of the Home)

And the Lord God took the man, and put him into the garden of Eden to dress it and to keep it (Genesis 2:15 KJV).

The English word *husband* comes from the Old Norse word *husbondi* (house bond or band), referring to "a freeholder, the superintendent or owner of a house or of property." He is the master, the manager, the owner, the operator, the caretaker, the cultivator, the protector, and the provider. The husband bonds or bands the house (home) together.

Husbandry began in the garden of Eden when God told Adam to "dress" [*abad*] and "keep" [*shamar*] the garden. The

Hebrew word *abad* means "to work, to cultivate, to serve, to till, to dress." "Husbandman" means "to keep, to labor, to bring to pass."[13] The Hebrew word *shamar* means "to hedge about (as with thorns), i.e., to guard; generally, to protect, attend to."[14] It is a man's responsibility to protect and defend his home.

Man also has the responsibility to *work* or cultivate and protect the marriage—to keep it bonded together and in good repair. Most people resist the bonds of covenant in marriage. They wrestle with a desire to be free and without responsibility to another. The truth is that a person cannot be married *and* totally free.

My wife, Gina, and I are not as free as we were when we were single. We have faced the fact that marriage and family are an inconvenience to our self-centeredness. Accept it, don't resist it, and do not complain about it. It is part of the responsibility of the marriage union and covenant!

I know I must put my wife ahead of myself, and prefer her over myself. I must inconvenience myself for her welfare, and it is my responsibility to protect her with my life if necessary. Her commitment to me is similarly binding.

I was just the male in my house before I was married. Now I am a *husbondi*. I am responsible for binding the marriage together and cultivating it to prevent *di*vorce. As the head, I must prevent *divorce* (di, meaning two), that is, two forces opposing each other. *Di*version is two versions opposing, and *di*vision is like two visions in dissonance with each other.

A husband can cultivate and lead his house without acting like a dictator. When he binds and restrains everyone else in the family, he himself is restrained. The marriage bond should be a loving commitment. It is a duty and obligation imposed by a contract, promise, or agreement that both parties enter into by *choice!* The contract is both spiritual and legal. You are restrained by God from having illicit affairs. You are restrained by the law of love and by the law of the land from beating or abusing your wife.

The Differences Between Men and Women

Many of the problems that plague marriages from the beginning stem from the basic biological differences between men and women. Pastors Brent and Janis Sharpe, in charge of counseling in our local church, shared some statistics with me about some of the differences between men and women that helped me better understand what usually is "the battle of the sexes."

According to their account, which is based on Dr. Donald Joy's figures,[15] for every 125 males conceived, 100 females are conceived. For every 105 males born, 100 females are born. For every 100 living 18-year-old males, there are 100 living 18-year-old females. The imbalance changes dramatically as males and females age. For every 44 males older than 85, there are 88 females over the age of 85—then the ratio is two-to-one!

Even the birth and mortality tables prove that the male seed is attacked by satan from the moment of conception. Why? They are the key to the protection of the race and the headship of the household. This is a profound truth, and far too little attention is given to it.

Thirty-three percent more males than females die in the first year of life, probably because females are born with a better immune system to help them later protect unborn children in the womb.[16]

While females are more sensitive to pain due to a more extensive tactile nervous system, they also have a higher threshold of pain than men to help them handle labor in childbirth. In other words, she can tolerate continuous pain for longer periods of time.[17]

A male has 50 percent more brute strength than a female, and his strength increases from puberty to 30 years of age. The female's strength peaks at the age of 12 and then levels off.[18]

Males have one and a half gallons of blood, while females have four-fifths of a gallon of blood; and the male heart delivers oxygen 20 percent faster. The male heart beats eight times slower than that of females, but the female's blood pressure is ten points lower.[19]

The male has thicker bones, while the female hears better. The male sees better in the light, while the female sees better in the dark. In general, a woman has better sensory perception than a man.[20]

Females have a layer of insulating fat cells to help them insulate and protect the womb, so it is harder for them to lose weight, and easier to gain a few pounds.[21] If men were as concerned about protecting their wives' feelings as God is, and if they would insulate them with faith like God insulated them with fat, then their wives would always be precious and beautiful to them!

Women have the ability to see things differently from men. A male's memory is designed to retain only the information that has a specific relation to him. He is more self-centered. The female, on the other hand, stores a wider variety of information. She tends to notice the little things, the details that men overlook. It has been most fascinating since I've been married to notice how my wife can always find the tiny little things I never can: tiepins, wallets, keys, etc. She rarely sees the big picture, as I do, but she sure can keep tabs on or recover the details.

A Difference in the Brain

The most profound distinction between men and women is the physiological difference in their brain development. Prenatal brain development and physiology affect how we think, learn, see, smell, feel, communicate, love, make love, fight, succeed, or fail. Between 18 and 26 weeks of gestation, testosterone and other hormones flood the body of male preborns, causing the *corpus callosum*—the connective tissue between the two hemispheres of the brain—to disintegrate significantly. This tissue provides the electrical links that promote cognitive intercommunication between the left and right hemispheres of the brain.

In contrast, female newborns do not experience this profusion of male hormones, and the *corpus callosum* in their brains remains totally intact. The net result is that males tend to become "lateral thinkers" who concentrate their thought on only one side of the brain at a time (switching between the analytical and the creative functions, respectively). Females, however, have a greater ability to cross over and think "bilaterally"—using both sides of their brains at the same time. At times it seems they are almost schizo because they generally see both sides of a situation or matter and occasionally appear confused as to their opinion, whereas men in their lateral thinking appraisals tend to see it only one way (their way). Therein lies the substance of sometimes extreme arguments.

Another noteworthy biological distinction is that the male's strength allows him to carry out tasks regardless of how he feels. He is work-oriented. The combination of his single focus and physical strength, triggered by the higher levels of testosterone in the womb, allows a man to press forward with single-minded determination and greater physical strength to achieve specific goals.

Perhaps the greatest motivation for this performance-oriented focus is that males derive their self-esteem from accomplishing a task. Females, on the other hand, primarily draw their self-esteem and strength from relationships.

Women are relationship-oriented with a deep need for intimacy. Satan used this need to deceive Eve in the garden when he established a relationship by talking to her while Adam was probably somewhere working in the garden.

How Men and Women Communicate

After Gina and I had enjoyed a short time of life as newlyweds, I began to notice that she continually said things like, "Honey, let's talk," or "Sweetheart, we need to talk more—we don't communicate (converse) enough." I've also learned that when women speak, they are usually saying what they feel, whereas when men speak, we are generally saying what we think. Society has taught men not to express or even acknowledge emotions or feelings; we therefore tend to secretly or even inadvertently internalize our deepest sentiments, be they positive or negative. This tendency to reserve our feelings sometimes builds and festers to an uncontrollable boil, which sooner or later resurfaces in frightful and often violent outbursts, leaving in their wake ugly pain and injury.

I have always said that the more you talk, the less you need to talk. What I mean by that is, "*Communication* (verbal interaction) *leads to communion* (oneness, intimacy, or fellowship)."

Women are communicators. They not only like to talk in general (as a pleasurable pastime), but it is my observation that they also "need" to talk. They use both sides of their brain to generate and exchange an average of 25,000 words a day, compared to the male's average of only 12,000 words per day! Sixty percent of a woman's words tend to be personal and relational, compared to only 23 percent of a man's words.[22] If you have not noticed already, men tend to "notice the headlines," while women notice the "line-by-line detail."

Since my son's birth, however, I have found plenty of details to talk about with others! I have not been able to resist the old "spirit of competition" so common to proud papas. Several of our friends, including various couples in our church, had babies around the time our son was born. Since then, I have found myself continually comparing my son's development with that of other boys and girls his age.

I entered my son in every "competition" I could think of, from teething, weaning, and potty training, to the more exotic events of walking, talking, and motor skills. I love teaching my son to say new words and then telling my friends of his progress. Although my competitiveness over him will probably lessen in the years to come, I am told the "proud papa" condition never quite goes away.

A Harvard preschool study found that 68 percent of the sounds little boys make are actual words, while 100 percent of the sounds made by little girls are words.[23]

Boys intersperse their words with action sounds, such as the firing of a gun and the roar and growls of animals. In general, adult males love to watch action movies where they can still say things like "pow," "ugh," "vroom," and "boom"! Women, on the other hand, would rather see an emotional love story, because it is relational.

In my own limited research study, I have confirmed that the little Pearson male has mastered the art of the "pow, ugh, vroom, boom," plus an impressive variety of animal growls. His little female counterparts, however (who participated in my study free of charge, courtesy of their mothers), are somewhat ahead of him in verbal skills.

At first this tended to irritate me—after all, this was my boy—but I learned it is quite normal for most little boys to develop this way. I have been told by those who know that even I developed about the same way my son is progressing!

With these differences between the sexes, men usually deal with stress by withdrawing "to find solutions." We do not want to talk or be around a lot of people. Men prefer to just sit and think in their search of a logical solution to issues. Women prefer to "talk it out" with other people to feel better. They deal with stress by wanting to verbalize their problems. A woman's greatest need is for someone to listen.

In general, men are motivated by feelings of being needed (significant), while women are motivated by feelings of being cherished. A man fears failure; he is afraid that his project or work will not be good enough. A woman fears she will fail because she (personally) is not good enough! She believes failure would somehow prove that she does not deserve love. Satan always tries to make a woman feel she is not good enough.

Many husbands play right into the devil's hands by making their wives feel unloved because they fail to communicate their love. Men seem to constantly wrestle with relationships. Many times, the problems men have stem from the unhealthy relationships they had with their parents. These might include a domineering mother with a distant and uncaring father, or vice versa. Whatever the lack, they often carry its repercussions into their own marriages and other adult relationships.

The Search for Intimacy

One of the greatest frustrations for most men is their inability to be intimate with their wives to their own satisfaction—or hers. Our English word *intimacy* comes from the Latin and French derivatives suggesting "innermost or inward most."

Men and women have different definitions of intimacy. While men tend to believe intimacy is essentially sexual, women believe it is relational. Any man who wants intimacy with his wife should realize that *intimacy does not start in the bedroom*! It starts in the kitchen every morning when he kisses her on the cheek and warmly tells her how much he loves her. It starts with a listening ear and a sensitive heart as they draw aside and pray together. Believe it or not, one of the most intimate things a man can do is to pray with his wife! (Each partner leading interchangeably.) It brings unity and union of spirit.

Relationships require cultivation, and it is the man's responsibility to cultivate marriage. That is why, as we said earlier, God assigned husbands the first year to "cheer up" their wives. God did not think men needed cheering up because they had married, but He thought women did. They actually give up more and take on more than most of us men realize. Today, we seem to look at this differently. Society thinks men need consoling because they are not supposed to "play the field" or continue many of their bachelor ways, hobbies, and habits after marrying. As usual, the world's ways are opposite to God's ways.

Husband, make it your job to understand your wife and cultivate real intimacy with her, particularly when you are first married and establishing the pattern for future years.

Adam's Rib

So the Lord God caused the man to fall into a deep sleep; and while he was sleeping, He took one of the man's ribs and closed up the place with flesh. Then the Lord God made a woman from the rib He had taken out of the man, and He brought her to the man (Genesis 2:21-22).

The Lord put Adam into a deep sleep and removed one of his ribs. The Bible says God "closed up the place with flesh," and I believe that was the first time man's blood was shed. This marked the beginning of our blood covenant with God, and the woman is directly aligned to it! A few thousand years later, Jesus was pierced in the side under the rib cage. In essence, His Bride, the Church, also was taken "out of His side."

In John 19:34, when the Roman soldier's spear punctured the pericardia around the Lord's heart, "blood and water" poured out of the wound. Physicians say that this proves Jesus' heart had exploded. Jesus literally died of a broken heart.

Blood represents life, and water represents the Holy Spirit. Jesus had to bleed in order to reproduce Himself in His Bride, the Church, the Body of Christ. According to Scripture, "...without the shedding of blood there is no forgiveness" (Heb. 9:22).

God distinguished the woman by perforation, which required the same level of intimacy as the making and inspiration of the man, Adam. Unfortunately, Eve did not seem to understand that intimacy. She did not realize that she too had been made in the image of God. Yet God already had become one with her in the spiritual sense of the word. I believe satan made her feel she was less than Adam, so she ate from the forbidden tree.

Marriage should be a form of worship to God because it fulfills God's purpose for man and woman. It is supposed to be a duet in perfect unity and harmony, not a duel to the death. The word *flesh* used in Genesis 2:21-23, the Hebrew word *basar*, is derived from a word suggesting freshness or cheerfulness in content or message. According to *Strong's Concordance*, it is "a glad news or gospel." In other words, the unity of marriage preaches a form of God's unconditional love from which, as Romans 8:35-37 says, nothing can separate us. It is definitely a form of worship.

Note also the difference between *unison* and *unity*. Unison means sameness, whereas unity means harmony. Unison is strength, but not necessarily beauty. When Amos wrote, "Can two walk together, except they be agreed?" (3:3 KJV), he used the Hebrew word *yaad*. It means "to fix upon or meet together at an appointed time or place." It means "to engage or commit together or mutually."[24]

In Greek the word for "agreement" is *symphoneo*, from which we get our English word *symphony*. It literally means "to sound together (in harmony)." A symphony has several different instruments all playing together, or simultaneously, at various intervals.

The differences in marriage don't have to divide us; instead, they can be used to bring beauty and harmony to the exchange. The sound is wooing and worshipful.

Did you know that we get the word *hymn* from the word *hymen*? In some cultures, *hymen* means wedding song.

There's a direct association between the hymen and marriage with the worship of God. There's a sacredness in marriage just as there is in the worship of God

A man was born to work, but a woman was born to worship. When the worker and the worshiper come together, they complete and fulfill the purpose for which they were made.

The first time man probably bled was when Adam lost his rib. The first time Eve bled was very possibly when God punctured her through—broke the hymen—and she sang. I believe hymns flowed out of her, and if so, this further verifies worship in the blood. There is awesome intimacy in that hymn. It is a marriage song. Marriage should be a form of worship to God because it fulfills God's purpose for man and woman, and it typifies God's unconditional love and commitment to the human world He created.

Under God's guidance, there is a unity of the male and female. The devil is afraid of that union. He is jealous of the ability and freedom of godly husbands and wives to worship God in total unity, and in spirit and in truth. As Lucifer, the devil was the chief worshiper and musician in Heaven, but each time a husband and wife worship God in, through, and by marriage, satan knows he has been replaced forever!

Ribs Are Flexible

I think when Adam woke up, he felt a little one-sided because part of him had been removed. The English definition of "rib" is "any of the paired, curved, bony or partly cartilaginous rods that stiffen the walls of the body...and protect the viscera [internal organs]."[25]

Thus Eve had both strength and flexibility, like the rib. Women are not supposed to be so stiff that they will break if they bend. It is the man who is built to be stiff and solid like an oak tree. Women are more flexible. They bend like a palm tree in a storm, but straighten up essentially undamaged after a storm. God gave Eve, and all of her daughters, enough strength to stand, yet enough softness and flexibility to curve around a man. If both woman and man were rib-like, marriage would be much too weak to last; and if both man and woman were oak-like, marriage would have been only and continuously disastrous. Contrary to popular belief, God truly knew what He was doing.

The ribs of the human body form the protective walls that protect the delicate internal organs within. God made the first woman from Adam's rib, which guarded his deepest drives and emotions. The ribs protect the liver, the intestines, and the heart. In the same way, a man and woman unite in marriage for mutual protection and support.

While this was and is God's plan for man, something happened that removed Adam from his office as dresser and keeper of God's garden. It also altered the relationship of men toward women in a negative way that still affects us today! In the end, this event resulted in Adam and Eve's being cast from Paradise into the wilderness of the rest of the world to eke out a weary living among thorns and thistles.

This was the beginning of separation—from God and from each other.

This was the beginning of aloneness of spirit.

This was the beginning of man's desperate search to belong to something or someone.

This was the beginning of sorrow.

Chapter 3

The Woman
Thou Gavest Me

*The man said, "The woman You put here with me–she gave
me some fruit from the tree, and I ate it"* (Genesis 3:12).

The wedding ceremony is normally a time of great celebration and joy. However, the marriage itself can be a horse
of a totally different color. It is a serious and solemn embar-
kation of trust and responsibility.

From the beginning man has tended to point his finger
of blame at anyone available, especially his wife, to verify or
excuse his own reactionary faults.

My initial engagement to Gina, with all its infatuation and
intrigue, caused me to boast quite profusely of the love, joy,
and grace God had brought into my life. However, once the
wedding was over and the real solemnity of the responsibility
of mutual sharing and submission began to enforce its miles,
my tendency was to blame both God and my wife for whatever
discomforts, inconveniences, or frustrations I encountered.

When I first met my wife, I saw her as a gift from God to me
and said so repeatedly. After a few confrontive challenges, I

found myself saying to God something similar to what Adam said in a moment of defensive despair: "This woman Thou gavest me!"

I often tell men in my ministry travels, "If you are having trouble with your wives, you are not alone. God is having trouble with His—that is us, the Church!"

Scripture refers to the Church as the Bride of Christ (see Jn. 3:29; Rev. 21:2). The inference is that God has made a heavenly commitment to His people that is similar to the earthly relationship between the husband and his wife. It is as sacred and as binding as our biblical covenant in marriage. The apostle Paul wrote that the relationship and attitude of a husband to his wife should be "modeled" after the relation of Christ to His Church (see Eph. 5:25-32).

We also are told that God "hates" divorce (see Mal. 2:16). Notice that only six chapters into Genesis, we find God already repenting (literally, "sighing ruefully") over having made mankind. However, He did not divorce us. He simply ran some "bathwater" and cleaned up the earth. Noah, who lived through that time with his wife, three sons, and their wives, called it "a flood." Then God started all over again with *adom*, mankind.

Actually, all through biblical history, especially the Old Testament, God constantly displayed His unconditional love and commitment to the Old Testament church, Israel (His wife). It appears that God was in a constant effort to keep Israel from backsliding to false gods and idols: "Turn, O backsliding children, saith the Lord; for I am married unto you" (Jer. 3:14a KJV). He refers to his idolatrous relationships as adultery. Hosea 3:1 says, "The Lord said, to me, 'Go, show your love to your wife again, though she is loved by another and is an adulteress'...." Notice that word *again*; it suggests tolerance, patience, and repetition.

God uses the entire Book of Hosea to show us how a husband's love for his wife, marriage, and family must remain consistent and repetitious throughout. In chapter 1 of Hosea, the prophet is instructed by God: "...Go, take to yourself an adulterous wife and children of unfaithfulness, because the land [Israel, the Church, or God's wife] is guilty of the vilest adultery in departing from the Lord" (Hos. 1:2). I'm not in any way suggesting here that all wives or women are adulteresses or adulterous; neither do I believe God's intentions are to put women or the female in an unfavorable light. He is, however, proving His husbandly and fatherly love of the Church. He is portraying through Hosea's experiences how a husband and father should and must continue to allure, support, forgive, recapture, recover, and defend what is his sacred trust and responsibility in and to his family and his wife.

Remember the flood in Genesis? There's something unique and special about running bathwater for your wife. Paul says in Ephesians 5:25-26, "Husbands, love your wives, just as Christ loved the church and gave Himself up for her to make her holy, cleansing her by the washing with water through the word." If you as a husband man don't know or have enough Word to wash (bathe) your wife, you are handicapped and severely disadvantaged.

Based on my personal experience, you can run a tub full of warm water, sprinkle bath beads in it, turn the lights down or off, light candles, and play some soft music for your wife, and that will solve almost any problem—at least temporarily. In the right spirit, you can do the same with the Word of God.

From Innocent Obedience to Self-Will

In the beginning, Adam and Eve were both naked and felt no shame. That means they were completely open to one another; they had nothing to hide (see Gen. 2:25). That is the way God intended marriage to be. Men and women were not created to attack and fight one another, but to love, share, and cooperate with each other in marriage.

According to biblical chronology, Eve had not yet been created when God told Adam not to eat from the tree of the knowledge of good and evil (see Gen. 2:16-17).

When the devil began to confuse her with "loaded" questions to which he already knew the answers, she should have said, "Adam, sweetheart, come and give me an interpretation of what this serpent is saying." (Evidently it was not uncommon for serpents to speak.) "He is questioning God's instructions to us! Would you answer him for me, please?"

Instead, Eve went her own way, and Adam apparently watched Eve and the serpent and did nothing about it. At this point, Adam should have intervened, saving her and all of us.

Even today, I am very particular about whose thoughts, voices, and philosophies are influencing my wife. She is too influential with me to remain unprotected by me in her relationships outside of and in addition to our marriage.

If this sounds "domineering," then remember that the "Me Generation" made a fetish of independence from all authority, even God's, and that is why this country is in the mess it is. It may be well to understand that throughout eternity, whether you are in Heaven or hell, someone is going to be over you in authority or rank. Only God has no higher authority. Right now, even those who do not obey God and think they are "free and independent" are really following the authority of a hidden "boss"—the serpent from Eden, who is still among us.

I am not talking about choosing my wife's friends for her. I am talking about remaining sensitive to the leading of the Holy Spirit concerning people who might try to influence me through her. At the same time, she is alert for people who might take advantage of me. A husband and wife should care enough about each other to share their feelings about each other's important relationships outside of marriage. If they do, a powerful defense mechanism is put in place for that couple that no foe can assail.

If Adam had exercised strength and resolve, it would have been both a powerful witness and a powerful deterrent to the serpent's enchanting seductions. I believe many women are desperately wanting their husbands to be as resolute in their purposes as the serpent was in his. Perhaps there is something strongly appealing to a woman about a man who knows his God, knows his purpose, and is prudent in his personal resolve.

God had spoken directly to Adam and had nurtured him. They had somewhat established covenant through their interactive relationship, as is indicated by God's questions to Adam after He found him hiding among the trees in the garden:

"Who told you you were naked?" (Its inference is…)

"Who have you been talking to in addition to Me?"

"Did you eat from the forbidden tree?"

"Have you been living off information and influence not ordained by Me?"

Apparently Eve allowed the serpent to establish an ongoing relationship with her that ultimately had devastating repercussions on the entire planet and all of its inhabitants.

She took the fruit, ate it, and gave it also to her husband who was with her, the Bible says (see Gen. 3:6).

I am sure Eve gave Adam one of those "looks" that only a wife can give her husband—the kind that says, "Oh, go on and take it, you big baby! It won't bite you."

Despite what God had told him, Adam knowingly rebelled and also ate of the fruit. He chose his wife over God. That is why God dealt more harshly with Adam than with Eve. God had specifically told Adam not to eat from that tree (and in the very next verse, Genesis 2:18, He said it was not good for man to be alone).

The Bible does not say God told Eve the same thing concerning the tree. It is likely He intended for Adam to "fill her in" on all that had happened previously. It seems the only way for her to have learned about the warning was through Adam.

The devil, through this cunning, crafty serpent, dug out his old bag of tricks from the days when he had deceived a third of the angels in Heaven (see Rev. 12:3-4). He put on his finest snakeskin boots and "britches" and used all his twisted skills to deceive Eve into believing that God had said something He did not say.

He uses the same tired, tricky questions today—and they work far too often! Satan's trick question to Eve, as recorded in the Genesis account, is, "Did God say you can't eat of any of the trees in the garden?" Or, as he would word his deceptive questioning today:

"Did God say you Christians cannot enjoy life?"

"Did God say to go to church every day...all day...to pray to an angry and resistant God?"

"Did God say all women have to wear dull and boring clothes and that all Christians have to have long faces?"

"Did God say that His children must be so heavenly minded they are no earthly good?"

*"You will not surely die," the serpent said to the woman. "For God knows that when you eat of it your eyes will be opened, and you will be like God, knowing good and evil." When the woman saw that the fruit of the tree was good for food and pleasing to the eye, and also desirable for gaining wisdom, she took some and ate it. She also gave some to her husband, who was with her, and he ate it. Then the **eyes** of both of them were opened, and they realized they were naked; so they sewed fig leaves together and made coverings for themselves* (Genesis 3:4-7).

God did not say Adam and Eve must not touch the tree of the knowledge of good and evil. He told Adam they were not to eat of it. "For in the day that you eat of it you shall surely die" (Gen. 2:17b NKJ).

Satan carefully engineered his words to confuse Eve, saying, "Surely you will not die." Eve didn't even understand death, because no one had ever died before. It is possible that even no animal had died. When God told Adam they would die, what could that have meant to them?

The word *die* in its scientific definition literally means "to fall out of correspondence with." It does not necessarily mean "to be extinguished," but instead, it means "to be destroyed, de-structured." Satan cannot extinguish the human race, even though he has made continued unsuccessful attempts to do so through wars, famine, and disease. He is the author of the many dreaded incurable diseases that mankind has been susceptible to over the centuries.

The closest thing to extinction the devil can impute to humanity is the destruction and fragmentation of the races. He wins by dividing husband and wife, parents and children, brothers and sisters, friend from friend, and race from race. The first murder on this planet was of a young man by his brother (see Gen. 4:8-12). Cain was jealous of Abel's pleasing God by his obedience in worship.

Cain said, "I'll worship You, God, but I'm going to do it my way."

That is never acceptable to God. That is "religion." If satan cannot stop us from worshiping, he will do his best to keep us from worshiping in unity and togetherness. Since the Garden of Eden, he has successfully perpetuated his tactic of "divide and conquer." He is the father of lies, a liar from the beginning (see Jn. 8:44). In essence, Jesus said that when satan lies, he is speaking his "native language."

Blinded by a Lie

Satan beguiled Eve into believing she would "be like God" if she ate the forbidden fruit. The truth was that her eyes could only be "opened" to the knowledge of good and evil through *disobedience*. The very instant she disobeyed God's command, her innocence and purity died forever. Her spiritual eyes were closed to God!

She and her husband lost their privilege of intimate fellowship with the Creator and their ability to behold God's glory. As a result, they never got to eat from the tree of life, which stood right next to the forbidden tree (see Gen. 3:22).

Diabolical Distortion: Deception

The god of this age has blinded the minds of unbelievers, so that they cannot see the light of the gospel of the glory of Christ, who is the image of God (2 Corinthians 4:4).

The Hebrew word for "serpent" is *nachash*. It means "to hiss, i.e., whisper a (magic) spell...enchanter."[26] The main Greek term used in the New Testament for "snake" is *ophis*. It has the same root as *optomia*, which means "to look at, or behold."[27] The English term, *ophthalmology* comes from the same root. From the beginning, the hissing enchantments of the serpent have been directed toward our vision and focus. The enemy of our souls is determined that we miss the target, goal, and mark of God's calling and purpose.

The serpent constantly hisses his enchantments to beguile your vision so you will lose sight of who you are. His object is to blind your eyes, or at least obscure your vision! That is why God said, "*Ish* [Man], I give you power to *tread upon serpents*" (see Lk. 10:19). He was saying that He was giving man a route—a track—over the devil's head. When a man walks the path God has given him to walk, he will crush the hissing serpent's head under his feet.

In my house, I am considered by both my wife and myself as the "Keeper of the Gate." I am the "watchman on the tower walls." I make up the hedge we spoke of earlier. I do not expect my wife to do warfare as I do.

Many women with nonspiritual husbands do engage in warfare, but they sustain the kind of spiritual injuries and wounds that do not easily heal—and may never properly do so. Therefore these women are crippled and handicapped in performing their other ordained womanly functions.

At times, my wife in her emotional sensitivity tends to be more acutely discerning of certain evil spirits attempting to use people around us in conspiracies against me. Immediately, and sometimes quite adamantly, she warns me of them. At those times, I must be careful not to let her emotional agitation distract me from what she has legitimately discerned. I must listen carefully and prayerfully, and then go immediately to battle against the approaching enemy.

Very often, a godly woman who is free to be what she is called to be in the home discerns many things. Sometimes it is pride, ego, and impenitence in her husband! Sometimes it is rebellion being stirred up in the children of the home, and sometimes it is seducing spirits outside the home. Whatever the situation, it is a sensitive husband's God-ordained responsibility and equipping to head off the threat and protect his household. He is the "house bondsman" or hus-band, as we have already discussed.

Stand in the Gap!

Women are not called or equipped to crush the devil's head on the front lines in the same way men are. Although they have all the armor of God, the gifts of the Spirit, and equal access to the presence of God, their assignment and makeup are different. Not only do women bear young and nurture them in safety, but they also are anointed to lift up their men while the men do battle in obedience to God's assignment.

Every woman should be praying for her man and nurturing him in the pursuit of his calling instead of putting him down. Michal, King David's first wife, refused to support or cooperate with him in worshiping God as he returned the ark of the covenant to Jerusalem after its 70-year exile in Philistia. God brought barrenness on her for the rest of her life because of her dishonoring attitude toward her husband. (See Second Samuel 6:16, 20-23.)

Again, the woman did not come from the man's head to be over him, or his feet to be under him, but from his side to be near him. God took her from Adam's rib cage, which functioned as protection for the tenderest organs in the chest cavity, primarily the heart.

When I met Gina, I was well along in life and in hot pursuit of my recognized destiny. The church I pastor was strong and growing stronger. My evangelistic organization was strong and prosperous. I had, in my opinion, a clear vision of both who I was and where I was going—or at least where I thought I was going!

Some of the earliest challenges in our marriage involved a mutual recognition and identification of Gina's role in support of my vision. In effect, she had to learn her role as "a rib" (not to "rib" me or nag me), but in effect, to cover and buttress me, to support my heart.

It is a wife's responsibility to know what is in her husband's heart and to guard it as a sentinel. As Gina and I came into this revelation, we both began to value her role and function in our home with a higher regard and respect.

When a woman prays for her mate, God hears her and is well pleased. When she sings and worships her Creator, God hears her and blesses her house. Remember, we have called her the worshiper along with her husband, the worker.

When women uphold men in prayer, men start looking for devils to defeat! They will charge to the front lines! A woman's travail and prayer will birth a courage and a spiritual authority in her man that will make him bold enough to charge hell with a water pistol!

When women go to prayer, they will see their husbands come out of hiding and stop running away from responsibility. They will see men stop siring babies out of wedlock. These men will rise up out of their enchanted blindness with eyes that are open! Their focus will become clear as never before! The dedicated prayers of women will make the men in their lives stand tall to make up a wall and bridge the gap!

The devil cannot stand it when men are in their place, so he will use every means he can to twist and distort their relationships with women and other men. His assault weapons include homosexuality, lesbianism, abortion, and a host of other perversions.

Many leaders in the church world—*supposedly our prophets*—sanction these perversions because of the fear of men, or because of their own sinful desires. Countless pastors are leading God's people astray in the name of Christ, but in total rejection of the commands of Christ.

Modern "secular prophets" are declaring, "This is the way—follow me in it!" These include godless politicians, leaders, school principals, and even parents.

The ancient spirit of deception, *nachash* (Hebrew), or *ophis* (Greek), is still whispering and hissing enchantments in our land, causing many of America's "prophets" to spout diabolically inspired lies in the name of political correctness, philanthropy, or humanitarianism. This is not of God! Every word of God is true, and in complete agreement with every other word He has uttered and preserved in the Bible. Worst of all, when a *true prophet* lies, when a God-anointed and appointed leader who names the name of Christ lies to the people, it brings God's wrath!

> *Her priests...do not distinguish between the holy and the common; they teach that there is no difference between the unclean and the clean.... Her officials within her are like wolves tearing their prey; they shed blood and kill people to make unjust gain. Her prophets whitewash these deeds for them by false visions and lying divinations. They say, "This*

is what the Sovereign Lord says"–when the Lord has not spoken (Ezekiel 22:26-28).

False prophets are deceiving the Church even as the serpent—who in my opinion was the first false prophet, or psychic—lied to Eve in the garden! I do not care how good a prophecy sounds. I do not care how "positive" it sounds. If God did not say it, it is a lie. *Just because something is a good idea does not mean it is a God-idea. We've been lied to far too long!*

Notice how Eve viewed the forbidden fruit. When the woman saw that the fruit of the tree was "good for food" (lust of the flesh, 1 Jn. 2:16 KJV), "pleasing to the eye" (lust of the eyes, 1 Jn. 2:16 KJV), and "desirable for gaining wisdom" (the pride of life, 1 Jn. 2:16 KJV), she ate it (Gen. 3:6).

Satan, in his deception, always appeals to our base, or lower, nature with its appetites and lusts. The serpent presently lives off the dust from which all mankind was formed. He has a definite objective and is operating according to his own devilish agenda.

Lovers of Money

The conspicuous lack of reverence for God is breaking apart our society. Many of our leaders are like wolves tearing at their prey. Too many followers are lovers of money more than lovers of God. Scripture says the love of money is the root of all evil (see 1 Tim. 6:10 KJV).

Many circumstances that we blame on racism are not really caused by racism at all. Slavery was a result of man's greed, but we have reduced it to a "black and white" issue. In reality, it was an economic issue. Throughout history, there were other races or peoples besides the black race who were enslaved, and in each case, the motive was not racism or sexism alone, but greed, avarice, and selfish ambition.

Today, a whole group of people are enslaved by poverty, and it has nothing to do with color. The *absence of a man in the home* is one of the primary causes of poverty! According to *U.S. News and World Report* (February 27, 1995):

"The absence of fathers is linked to most social nightmares—from boys with guns to girls with babies. Some 46 percent of families with children headed by single mothers live below the poverty line, compared with 8 percent of those with two parents."

The love of money causes lawyers to advertise on television that you can get a $45 divorce! Marriage and the male in particular are under assault by the enemy! The nuclear family is under assault, and people are confused. They do not know what to do. The Supreme Court's rulings suggest to them that abortion can fix their problem, and the government tells them it is okay and pays for the procedure!

The people of the land practice extortion and commit robbery; they oppress the poor and needy and mistreat the alien, denying them justice (Ezekiel 22:29).

The words of Ezekiel have come to pass in our generation! "Extortion" means to twist or to torture—literally, to force the hand of the innocent through intimidation and fear, and to commit robbery. Burglaries have become a runaway national plague. Every day, immigrants are denied justice and fair hearings, and the poor and needy live in cardboard houses on the streets of our concrete cities.

During a recent presidential convention, politicians from one national party paid homeless veterans to march and parade, hoping to create the impression that their party had "more compassion for the homeless" than the rival political party. After the parade was over, the homeless men were returned to a homeless shelter. This party spent $32 million on its national convention, but only gave each of the homeless men $500. Something is wrong. Look around carefully. You will probably discover that someone is trying to deceive you!

Wake up, Church! Get the Word into your heart! Find out what the Holy Ghost is saying! Do not believe false prophets. We have the Greater One living within us, and we should be listening to what He has to say, not to what politicians are saying.

Extortion Produces a Twisted Society

There are religious leaders who also tell a man it is okay to love another man, saying religiously, "After all, God made homosexuals the way they are."

It is a lie! God did not make any human being to have sexual relations with the same gender (see Rom. 1:26-27). From the destruction of Sodom and Gomorrah down through New Testament days, God has made clear His disapproval over homosexuality and lesbianism. Sin is sin! Let us call sin by its name. Today, sexual sins are no longer even people's "problems," but "alternative lifestyles." We live in a twisted society. I want to be as sensitive as possible in the next chapter, as I deal with this subject. I have lost dear Christian friends to AIDS, and some of them were married with children. The state of public opinion today concerning what was considered immoral and even illegal some 20 years ago is cause enough to pause and ponder how we got here and where we are going.

Chapter 4

Welcome to the "Gender-Blender" Era

Because of this, God gave them over to shameful lusts. Even their women exchanged natural relations for unnatural ones. In the same way the men also abandoned natural relations with women and were inflamed with lust for one another... (Romans 1:26-27).

Androgyny is sweeping our nation's entertainment, art, and fashion culture. This "gender-blender" mentality is one of satan's most effective assault weapons. His goal is to confuse gender in our relationships, so that males cannot be distinguished from females (when God made an extra effort to give each gender its own "distinguishing marks").

Women are looking (and acting) like men, and men are looking like women. You cannot tell the difference between them in this generation by looking at clothes, hairstyles, or mannerisms—and many do not know the difference themselves!

Men don't know how to be men anymore because they don't have enough good examples to follow. They don't know whether to be like Sylvester Stallone or Michael Jackson! While both men are famous, neither is the ideal for Christians. We are told to be like Jesus!

There is a diabolical spirit at work in the entire entertainment business, hissing its enchantments to audiences through music, prime time television, and the mass media. The Church must rise up again in the name of Jesus and identify the imposter!

Bitter women by the thousands are coming to the conclusion that "men are not necessary"! Why? It is because men have stopped acting like men! Lesbianism is on the rise, and society is trying to force us to accept homosexuality as a proper "alternative lifestyle choice." Millions of people are unsure of their sexual identity, because the serpent has convinced them they can only be affirmed through the sexual desires of someone of their own sex.

Much if not all of it can be traced back to the lack of a good father image in the home. Many homosexual men subconsciously are looking for another man's approval *because they did not get it from their fathers.* Every youth needs a man whom he respects to tell him, in essence, that it is all right to grow up and be a man. He needs to be affirmed in his manhood. He needs male validation from his father.

Meanwhile, no one is willing to address the issue openly and declare what the Scripture says: "This is the way; walk in it" (Is. 30:21c).

The world thinks we are dangerous to society if we dare to speak out against homosexuality, calling us "homophobic" (afraid of same sex relationships). Modern and traditional society is still struggling with the almost "mystical" (in the sense of occult) fascination with same-sex relationships and even "marriages"!

As Christians with a biblical foundation for our perspective, we need to stand up and proclaim what the Scriptures say:

This day I call heaven and earth as witnesses against you that I have set before you life and death, blessings and curses. Now choose life, so that you and your children may live and that you may love the Lord your God, listen to His voice, and hold fast to Him... (Deuteronomy 30:19-20).

I'd like to repeat in this chapter for you an excerpt from the fairest commentary I've read on this subject:

"Homosexuality is not so much a sin as a lie that cannot abide the manly Sword of Truth" (Gordon Dalbey).

"The incarnation (in-flesh-ment) of God in Jesus Christ reflects the basic truth that spiritual relationship seeks a physical component in this world. A boy's spiritual relationship with his mother is graphically 'enfleshed' in her womb—yet the boy also longs for a display of physical affection to complement his spiritual bond with his father.

"As Robert Bly puts it, 'A son has a kind of body-longing for the father, which must be honored.'

"In fact, the boy's body-longing for his father may be even more intense than that for his mother, since the boy has had nine months of intimate physical contact with her from conception. In any case, the boy needs his daddy to hold him, to hug him, even to tumble and wrestle with him on the living room floor.

"If, however, the father is physically cold or distant, or absent altogether, the boy's longing goes unfulfilled, and prompts anxiety about bonding with other males. In some cases, the boy suppresses in his subconscious the unbearable pain of not having the father's physical affection—only to have that longing resurface later in a distorted form: sexual desire for other men.

"It is not a sin to be born of a possessive mother and a distant father, nor to have consequent homosexual fantasies. It is a sin, however, to refuse to surrender yourself to Jesus and let God begin to shape you into His image as a man!

"To bring a prophetic word against homosexuality: One must confess at the Cross this longing for true and appropriate manly affection, and let Jesus lead one to the Father for healing—not hide it behind an aggressive anti-homosexual stance. There are men with 'homophobia.' They are the ones who are strongly repressing their 'father needs' and, sometimes, latent homosexual tendencies.

"If the conservatives' so-called sin is that they have fancied themselves 'more judging than God,' the liberals' sin is that they have fancied they could be 'more kind than God.'

"As an analogy, consider a conservative surgeon, who curses the patient, slashing him ruthlessly in an attempt to cure him, while a liberal doctor glibly pronounces the sick patient 'healthy' to spare him the pain of surgery. Neither has truly helped the patient. Either treatment actually may kill him!

"Declaring homosexuality to be healthy is therefore a quick-fix verbal cosmetic which may get fathers off the hook temporarily and save the son from the difficult work of looking honestly at himself. But men today who are distraught by sexual feelings for other men do not need to be told they are healthy nor do they need to be 'damned' to hell.

"They need to be told, instead, that God loves them and has come in Jesus Christ to set them free. They need to know they can be true sons of the eternal Father and true men in the image of Christ, hiding nothing and hiding from nothing."[28]

The opposing views, philosophies, or worldviews, that began in Eden are culminating in today's society: God's ways versus satan's ways. The result of this clash of truth and deception is mass confusion.

Men Are Confused—and So Are Women!

I believe strongly in femininity, but since the advent of the feminist movement, men are at a loss over such simple things as whether to open a door for a woman anymore.

Will they be called a "sexist" for doing a polite act?

Is being a gentleman politically incorrect? Does it make us seem feminine?

The continuous hissing of the enchanting serpent has made its mark on our society. Men do not know what to do to be a man anymore. They do not know what is right, or how to please women. It has become increasingly unpopular to be strong and masculine. Most of us men spend more time on our appearances than we did in the past. In fact, many men spend as much time looking in the mirror as their wives. Now, I'm not saying this is wrong; I'm simply saying it is different.

On the other hand, in previous ages, men in general dressed more dramatically than women did, or at least as much so. Only since Queen Victoria's reign, beginning in the mid-1800's, have men dressed in long trousers and dark colors. In the 1700's, men wore knee britches and colored tights, and women spoke openly of men who had "a well-turned leg."

What has driven men to wearing earrings, jewelry, and long hair again?

Are we "reverting to type"—that the male of the species was created to be more decorative—or are we reacting against the oppression of the extreme feminist movement?

Have we been so influenced by the philosophy of a reprobate society that we are uncomfortable being men in our own homes, so that we strive for importance outside the home?

What is it that makes men feel we have to do more, or do something else, to affirm our identities?

God is asking men again, "Who told you that you were naked? Who said you were inadequate and less than a complete man?"

Why do we spend so much time trying to feel good about ourselves? What convinced us to work so hard to "feel good" about ourselves? Most men feel inadequate as lovers, fathers, and husbands.

Where is the man in your house? Before you answer that question, answer these two first: *Where is the man in your head, and where is the man in your heart?*

Three Steps to Victory

Right thinking, right believing, and right speaking are the three steps to the integrated personality necessary for all Christians to be victorious.

Moral corruption and social injustice go hand in hand. No truly great humanitarian continually violates the laws and standards of chastity, purity, and virtue. Unbridled indulgence in the carnal appetites of the flesh produces selfish exploitation in both the moral and ethical realms.

The Greek word for "character" is *ethikos*. It's also where we get our Greek "ethics." It's the discipline of dealing with right and wrong, good and bad. Ethics refers to the set of moral principles, standards, and values that guide our conduct. A person with good character is someone who cares how he acts.

In our society, ethics have become "situational," meaning our standards of conduct change with each new situation or circumstance. The "new" ethics assumes there are no moral absolutes or fixed standards of right and wrong. When moral absolutes are ignored, there is no limit to the depths of depravity to which a person, a community, a society, or a nation will sink. However, right worship and right living are inseparable.

When our leaders—especially religious leaders—lower their standards, the people they lead lose all sense of discipline, control, and decency. They plunge headlong into the lewdest and lowest of vices. *Pornography* is one of the foul epidemics spawned by compromise, and it has infected men of every color, class, and creed.

We Are Facing a "Holy Meltdown"

God will consume America's filth with the fires of judgment. *His purpose is never punitive*, although at times it seems to be. God's ultimate purpose in judging sin is to correct and heal the sinner. He wants to separate the "dross" or useless things from the holy, just as ore smelters melt raw ore to obtain pure metals from an otherwise worthless mixture.

God is looking for men—intercessors and spiritual leaders—who will act as His representatives to hold back the tide of inevitable judgment, even if only temporarily. God is patient, but He is urgently searching this land for men to stand in the gap so judgment will not fall on this nation! America will never be what it was intended to be unless, or until, we repent.

Out of the dross and dregs of God's fiery judgment—I call it a *holy meltdown*—a purged and purified Church will arise, with a value more priceless than gold.

Our society is crying out, "Is there a man in the house?"

The path of pain goes all the way back to Eden. Just as the serpent hissed enchantments into Eve's ear to distort her view of herself, so he wants to distort your view of your mother and father. He wants to distort your own motherhood or fatherhood, and he whispers that your manhood or womanhood is "naked" and inadequate. He distorts, twists, and tortures the truth to get us off balance.

The adversary heard God say, "It is not good for the man to be alone" (Gen. 2:18). Satan probably hissed to himself, "What is not good? I want to know what is not good." Although the fallen angel was unable to create anything himself, he had become skillful at distorting and twisting the truth of created things, and taking advantage of that which is not "good."

Chapter 5

Thorns and Thistles

To Adam [God] *said, "Because you listened to your wife and ate from the tree about which I commanded you, 'You must not eat of it,' cursed is the ground because of you; through painful toil you will eat of it all the days of your life.* **It will produce thorns and thistles for you,** *and you will eat the plants of the field. By the sweat of your brow you will eat your food until you return to the ground, since from it you were taken; for dust you are and to dust you will return"* (Genesis 3:17-19).

One of the special challenges I have faced in these early days of married life, is getting my wife to understand what I call the "thorns and thistles" syndrome of the working man.

Usually when I return home from my office at the church each day, my wife and son meet me at the garage door entrance. Gina has a sweet and welcoming smile on her face and Julian has the most precious expression on his, while making incredible little sounds in anticipation of the cuddling kisses and hugs he gets from his proud papa. The encounter can be most therapeutic and even healing as sometimes—even most times—I'm still emotionally perforated from the thorns and thistles I've experienced in the field of my work. The average person would think that the pastorate should be a most soothing and comfortable profession, one not to be included in the category where thorns and thistles are conspicuous. On the contrary, ministering can be one of the most demanding, confrontive, and even combative professions into which a person can be engaged.

As pleasant and as sweet as my wife and son's welcome home to me is, it does not change the agitation of the thorns and thistles sometimes devastating effect on me and the period of healing time it daily necessitates. Only now is my wife beginning to understand why and how I tend to experience occasional mood swings and her need to patiently adjust to them even as I do to her semi-regular times of special duress and need. It usually takes me about an hour to shift from the working mode to the family mode.

To deal with this particular "syndrome," I turn as always for scriptural explanation. The Hebrew words for thorns and thistles recorded in the Genesis account are defined similarly as something that causes distress and irritation, a prickly, almost piercing, and arguably a God-ordained satanic antagonism.

When God created mankind (Adam), He created male and female (see Gen. 1:27). A woman is a female man and a man is a male man. The male man is the primary giver and the woman (female) is the primary receiver, the physical anatomy of our bodies suggests as much.

My friend, Dr. Myles Munroe, says, "In general, when the woman (wife) gives to the man (husband) that which he has not already first given her, it is usually, as in the case with Adam and Eve (Gen. 3:6), forbidden fruit, and usually causes the fall or at least the failure of the man."

As the worker and the initiator, Adam was designed to *provide for or give to* his wife, but instead, she gave to him first. A wife returns to her husband that which he has first given to her, only she multiplies it:

> He gives her a house, and she gives him a home filled with nurturing love and warmth.

> He gives her groceries, and she gives him delicious and nourishing meals.

> He gives her seed, and she labors and travails to give him a legacy in his children.

Sometimes a man loves a woman so much that he will not guide and guard her as God commands. Actually, that is not real love. True love does what is best for the other person, not what is best for oneself. This same principle holds true in parenting. Proper discipline and firm corrective action is a true sign of love. The devil perverts love so much that sometimes men are not loving out of their hearts, but out of their sexual or emotional needs.

Adam loved Eve so much that he violated all his principles. Abraham agreed to Sarah's impatient solution to God's delay in producing a son, and had a son by her maidservant, Hagar. To this day, nations fathered by that son, Ishmael, are locked in bitter conflict with Abraham's children through Sarah's son, Isaac.

The Taste of Dust

> *Then the Lord God said to the woman, "What is this you have done?" The woman said, "The serpent deceived me, and I ate." So the Lord God said to the serpent, "Because you have done this, cursed are you above all the livestock and all the wild animals! You will crawl on your belly and you will eat dust all the days of your life"* (Genesis 3:13-14).

Every creature, including man, came from the dust. Woman alone, among all living creatures, came from man and not from dust. Just as she should never know the thorns and thistles of a man's work, so she should never feel the bite of the gnawing serpent as would a man made of dust. She will be harassed by satan, but she will not be targeted for death as a man is.

And I will put enmity between you [the serpent] *and the woman, and between your offspring and hers; he will crush your head, and you will strike his heel* (Genesis 3:15).

God declared there would be perpetual enmity between the serpent and the woman and her seed. But He said Eve's male seed would crush satan's head, and the serpent would bruise or strike his heel. This bitter fight to the death reserved for Eve's male seed instigated an unending satanic attack on men (especially on the Messianic line before Christ came to earth).

The cross changed the rules laid down in Genesis. Jesus crushed satan's head on the cross and arose from the dead. Now any man who is covered by the blood of Jesus will give the serpent deadly heartburn every time he tries to take a nibble at his heel, because the snake can only taste Jesus! A man who goes into this battle must receive Jesus as his Lord if he is to survive and be victorious.

Sweat and Toil

The ground was not cursed because of woman, but because Adam abdicated his responsibility! Adam listened to his wife, and failed to do his part by throwing the hissing snake out of the garden. More than simply Adam's home, the garden was the place where he worked. He loved his job.

The harvest was plentiful, and all he had to do was pluck the ripe fruit off the trees. Life was good.

After Adam sinned, God told him his work would be changed into "painful toil." That is why men wrestle with employment today. It is their main focus and obsession. They get their security, identification, and personal gratification from their *work*. Yet it is also their biggest obligation, and it causes their greatest confrontations.

God said man would eat by the "sweat of his brow." The Hebrew word for "sweat" means "by vexation and agitation." Many men are abandoning their jobs, their wives, and their families because they have become frustrated over "the thorns and thistles of life" as it relates to their work or job. They get tired of taking care of the wife and children, so they leave the wife to bear the burden alone.

Thorns and Thistles Are Not for Women

To the woman He said, "I will greatly increase your pains in childbearing; with pain you will give birth to children. Your desire will be for your husband, and he will rule over you" (Genesis 3:16).

God did not tell the woman she would work among the thorns and thistles. He said she would have babies, which would be painful. (That was not God's original plan. Birth would have been an easier experience, if it hadn't been for sin.) He did not intend for woman to identify directly with the task of dealing with "thorns and thistles" any more than He meant for men to identify directly with the physical and emotional anxiety of childbirth.

Since then, the blood that once represented life has come to represent death. People are frightened by the sight of blood, and that is not what God intended. His Word says the life of every creature is in the blood (see Lev. 17:14).

The devil has twisted this truth around. That is why many churches have stopped preaching about the power of the blood of Jesus—it "offends" many people. Yet these same people, who shudder at the mention of blood from the pulpit, will sit in front of their televisions to watch hour after hour of violent, blood-spilling programs.

Blame a Backslidden Nation

Women were forced to enter the workforce each time America turned her back on God, causing the economy to slide. The Industrial Revolution spawned factories that took advantage of the cheap labor force of women and children who were overworked and underpaid.

At other times, ungodly speculation in gold, stocks, and bonds (another name for high-stakes financial gambling) undermined America's economy and birthed deadly depressions that forced entire families (women included) to work in factories and workplaces for low wages just to survive.

As I mentioned in the Introduction, world wars and costly global conflicts in this century pushed lonely women into factories, and their children into the hands of strangers, as the nation scrambled to build weapons and machinery for the men who were fighting on foreign soil.

After each major upheaval, two forces battled for control of the nation, the Spirit of revival and righteousness, and the spirit of godless pleasure-seeking and independence spawned by the horrors of war. Each time the prosperity and blessings of the Lord lifted, women had to go to work. Each time, society never returned to the previous traditional lifestyle, but continued to expand on the distortion from God's way.

Today, the "way to destruction" has been widened even more by a national rebellion against God and His righteousness.

It is almost impossible now for a family to exist on only one income from the husband. This is not God's plan—particularly when there are young children still at home. God never intended for our babies to be raised by strangers in day care centers. Many of our children return from these unnatural environments bearing the scars of sexual, physical, and emotional abuse!

I understand that today's circumstances demand much from women. But women, in general, simply cannot continue to fulfill the roles of both wife and breadwinner. It is killing them, and tearing their marriages apart! Being "freed" from the supposed drudgery of a housewife has not been a blessing but a curse. Women cannot exchange one role for another. Instead they end up trying to do both, which is not possible.

The Superwoman Syndrome

Janis Sharpe, a counselor, told the people in our services, "When the women's movement gave us the freedom to be *anything* we wanted, it required us to be *everything*": perfect woman, wife, mother, daughter, sister, worker, counselor, executive, administrator, and the list goes on.

Society has created a breed of women who look wonderful on the outside. They are physically fit, their homes look great, they're good moms, and they have good jobs. However, on the inside, these women are rapidly deteriorating! The impossible strain of trying to be "superwoman" has created an empty shell out of them! Many women are totally exhausted physically, mentally, and spiritually.

The "enchanter in the snakeskin boots" has been whispering again. The devil has used our twisted and distorted culture to convince women that nothing will ever be good enough. They are not good enough personally, and neither are their marriages, their families, their homes, their nails, their hair, their children, or their weight!

They buy the lie that *they must be perfect*. They have to be the perfect attorney, the perfect doctor, or the perfect preacher—all at the same time that they are trying to be the perfect wife, mother, homemaker, cook, and lover.

Women have left the home to enter the so-called "working world." They have climbed to the top of the corporate ladder, *but they still feel empty*! They are angry and exhausted, and they do not know why. The reason is that they have rejected and abandoned their primary call as married women, and that is to nurture husband and family, and manage the home.

My wife, Gina, does not work outside the home, but she is not a non-person. She has a head on her shoulders, and she has a full-time calling and occupation *in the home*. I make the final decisions, but I value her opinions. I honor and respect her, and we try to communicate with one another about everything.

Work Affirms Manhood

When the Russian Communists encouraged women to become doctors, they were shocked to see the medical profession in that country vacated by men! The profession was turned over to women, except in specialized fields. Why? Men have a clear tendency to abdicate responsibilities when women assume the leadership role. There is something in the nature God gave men that tells them it isn't right to compete and do battle with women; the conflict is unequal. We were created to protect and provide for women, not attack and divide.

It is not without significance that with the influx of women into the American workforce, *men have dropped out of many professions*! While females in the workforce have risen to nearly 40 percent, the percentage of males has dropped from almost 90 percent to just above 70 percent. Many of those men have joined the ranks of criminals, drug addicts, alcoholics, and the unemployed.

Carl Wilson, in his book, *Our Dance Has Turned to Death*, says that employers have long known that a good family man, who has a loving wife, is the best type of man to hire. If a man finds work that affirms his manhood and a woman who draws him to love her and build a family, he more than likely will become a valuable and constructive citizen.[29]

Ironically, another strange backlash has appeared on the horizon under the name of "sexual equality." If I take on the responsibilities of my wife at home, how does that validate me as a man? It doesn't. Men will become permanent "Mr. Moms" because of love or necessity, but they end up feeling less of a man. That does not mean a man should not help out at home, because he should! I am talking about men who are forced in some way to take on the full-time role of a homemaker so their wives can become the breadwinner. That may seem to work temporarily, but it eventually will backfire and become counterproductive, because it is basically against nature.

The State of the American Family

A study was conducted to find out what percentage of children in the United States were living with both parents, single parents, or non-parent guardians. The results are shocking. In 1960, eight out of ten American children lived with both parents in the home. Barely half live with both parents today! In 1960, less than eight in every hundred children lived with their mother alone. That number has skyrocketed to more than one in five today!

According to the same study, less than four in every hundred children lived with a parent who had never married in 1960. Today, nearly one out of every three children live with a mother who has never been married!

More than 82 percent of America's children lived in a home with their father in 1960. Today, less then 62 percent of America's children can say, "Daddy's home." More than a third of our children live apart from their fathers, and it is tearing our nation apart!

Even though this is a backslidden nation, most older Americans adhere to the biblical formula of the mother staying primarily in the home, while the father works outside the home. Just under 30 percent of all Americans under the age of 45 agree with the biblical pattern, but from 47 to 82 percent of those 45 years old and above believe the man should work while the woman should bear and nurture the young.

Parenting Has Its Seasons

Men sometimes wonder why they have to work and cannot spend more time with their children. While men should play an important role in their children's lives, their primary role is not taking care of the children. Instead, it is in making the overall provision for the entire household.

I was jealous of the time Gina spent caring for our son, Julian. I even tried to convince her to supplement Julian's breastfeeding with solid foods a month earlier than he was supposed to just so I could feel needed by my son! I wanted to feed him because I desperately wanted identity in my son's life. I wanted my son to recognize me. I wanted to feel significant to him.

I had to learn that parenting has its seasons. In the first few years of a child's life, God has ordained that the mother be the primary caregiver. I realize now that I will assume a more important role with my son later on (but I still have the impulse to "hurry things along"). My wife (the woman), is the primary caregiver in our home—where the husband man (me) is the primary caretaker.

Julian gets his breakfast, lunch, dinner, and in-between snack directly from his mother. Oh, I get to feed him a little bit once in a while, now that he has finally moved on to solid foods, but he still wants to be with his mother most of the time.

Honestly, I love my son so much that I would love to stay at home with him, but it is not God's plan for me. It is my job to go to work so that Gina will not have to worry about any-thing. My provision gives her security, and frees her to de-vote herself totally to the task of nurturing. This is not *my* plan; it is *God's plan.*

I want Gina to nurture Julian, but as a father, I also need to touch my son. I need to hold him, hug him, and kiss him. I need to validate him, and bond with him physically, emo-tionally, and spiritually. That is also an important part of God's plan.

Fairness Is Not Equality

As I mentioned earlier, "fairness" does not always mean "equality." When I get home, I help Gina around the house, but I don't do *half* the housework! My wife manages our home; I don't. I do some cooking, cleaning, and even laun-dry occasionally, but I do not do an "equal division of work."

No, I do my *fair share*. When I come home, I have put in a full day (or more) of hard labor in *my assigned tasks* at the church or on the road, just as Gina has put in a full day in *her assigned tasks* as nurturer and manager of our home. I see my role as the superintendent in our home and Gina as the manager; I'm the Chief Executive Officer where she's the Chief Operating Officer.

An article in the 1993 July/August issue of *Men's Health* magazine said, "On average, men generate nearly three-fourths of family incomes, and those earnings are reflected in hours on the job. Husbands usually work longer hours and travel farther to their jobs than wives do."

Many men were taught by example that the mother does everything around the house while the father does nothing. Men were only expected to go to work, but now there are men who not only expect their wives to do everything around the house, but hold down full-time jobs too! Sometimes women manage this feat, but it inevitably takes a toll on them and their marriage.

If a woman is a homemaker, then a man is a home-builder. However, if both the husband and wife work out-side the home, then there needs to be a *fair* division of the household chores. *Fairness is not equality.* My wife, Julian, and I eat fair, not equal, portions of food. Our individual appetites, tastes, and food intakes vary. It would be ludicrous to argue over equality. Spouses are always fighting for equality, but you cannot divide a child like an apple!

You cannot say, "I changed my son's diaper today, so you change him tomorrow," or "I bathed him today, so you bathe him tomorrow."

That is not God's plan. We are to love one another, care for one another, and help one another, but we should strive more for fairness than for equality.

Satan tempted Eve with the thought that she would be like or equal to God. God does not always give us equal portions, but He is always fair. We have trouble in our marriages because we demand equality. We should be working for fairness instead. Fairness requires justice, intelligence, and respect for one another. Equality has to do with a cold division of quantities without regard to function, appropriateness, or purpose.

Healing Is Possible

When the spirit of manliness rises up in the Church and men take their rightful headship by the Spirit, a mighty anointing will fall on the Body of Christ! A healing is coming to this nation, and deliverance is coming to God's people! But first, God is about to put our houses in order.

Chapter 6

The Destruction of Tomorrow

Therefore, if anyone is in Christ, he is a new creation; the old has gone, the new has come! (2 Corinthians 5:17)

Satan tries to destroy our future by offending us with our past. He loves to dig up the dirt from our roots, our lineage, and destroy our history. He causes us to doubt our purpose, our destiny, and our legitimacy, by causing us to question our significance with interrogations like:

"Why was I born the way I am?"

"Why was I born black, or red, or yellow?"

"Why was I born a man, or a woman?"

"Why was I not born someone else?"

"Why is everyone better than me?"

I have felt for years that God started the original "Azusa Street revival" in 1906 to eradicate the race problems in this country through a "Spirit-filled baptism of love and power."

God defied the social status quo of the time and brought blacks and whites together in a tremendous way through that great revival. But within three short years, those early twentieth century Christians had dropped the ball and gone their separate ways!

It took years for researchers and historians to find where William J. Seymour was buried. Seymour was the forgotten, one-eyed black preacher whose humility and dedication allowed Pentecost to be restored to the Church, the man God used to unleash that great outpouring of the Holy Spirit on Azusa Street in Los Angeles. Only in recent years has his contribution to that move of God been more fully appreciated.

Like a natural scavenger in the wild, satan has especially targeted the helpless and rejected for his vicious attacks through the memory of past wrongs.

Black women, perhaps more than the women of any other race on the face of the earth, have been exposed and subjected to vindictive satanic spirits by the conspicuous absence of their men! When a man is not in the home, the woman is vulnerable to spirits of anger, fear, rejection, loneliness, and even death.

According to the February 27, 1995, issue of *U.S. News and World Report,* 68 percent of the babies born to black women in this country are born outside of wedlock. Their so-called "men" have deserted them. That must stop! Any *male* can make babies, but it takes a *real man* to be a father!

Thirty percent of *all* babies are born outside of marriage. Why? Many of these babies are born to teenage mothers who desperately want love and attention. They got into trouble because of their inner need for male interaction and affirmation. As I mentioned earlier, if a girl does not get appropriate love and attention from her father, she will look for another male to give it to her.

Psychologists say that both male and female children get their sexual identity from the relationship they have with their father. If the father is absent, the daughter instinctively goes looking for another man!

In their book, *Growing Up With a Single Parent*, sociologists Sara McLanahan and Gary Sandefur maintain that teenage girls reared in divorced or disrupted families are *twice as likely* to become unwed teen mothers![30]

Blame the "Absentee Man"

Black and white women alike become frustrated and angry when they are forced to raise families without a man. They are trying to be Mama, Daddy, nursemaid, chauffeur, and counselor for their children all by themselves. They are overburdened and bitter, not to mention lonely.

When you see a woman rising up in anger, it is because *a man is not where he is supposed to be*! Somewhere along the line, a man has abandoned that woman in the lion's den of life to fend for herself. When she gets sassy, arrogant, vindictive, and sharp-tongued, she is actually taking on the nature of the serpent! But listen, I do not blame the woman; *I blame the "absentee man"*—her father or her husband!

You cannot have a "Jezebel" without an "Ahab" somewhere behind her, either as father or husband—or both. Ahab represents weak, indecisive, and irresponsible male leadership (see 1 Kings 16:31).

One of my young white friends said to me one time, "Carlton, black women are cute, but they seem to always have their hands on their hips! They always appear mad or upset about something!"

I told him, "That is because many of them *are* angry!" And many have ample cause to be angry.

From time to time, I hear black men say, "White girls are so nice. They are so much more feminine, and they seem to speak softer."

Perhaps they have not been beaten up, rejected, and abandoned as much as some black women! Of course this is a generalization, but we need to consider its implications nonetheless.

This Ain't 1960, Honey!

Back in the 50's and 60's, it was common for a black man to say to his girlfriend, "Say, Mama, you sure are fine. You know I really love you. I have been looking at you and thinking about you. I just need someone, you know, to stand with me in life. *I don't have a job, but I need someone to believe in me*...someone to help me get my G.E.D. certificate. You know, someone to *help me fill out my job applications*," etc.

The girl would say, "Well, I understand, because my mama stood with my daddy. My daddy didn't have nothin' either. My grandma stood with my granddaddy because, you know, he didn't have nothin'. And my great-grandmama stood with my great-grandpa because he was a slave. Let's get married. We ain't got nothin', so let's just have nothin' together!"

That may have gone over in the 60's, guys, but do not try that today! Most women, and black women in particular, are not going to take those old excuses from a man.

She will say, "You ain't got a what? You want me to fill out a what? You better get out of my face, and *get a job!*" Then she snaps her fingers with that typical circular arm rotation and speeds off in her brand-new, sassy red BMW.

On a more serious note, that attitude makes black men angry. It makes any man angry. But I don't blame the woman; I hold the man responsible. When Dr. Cole says, "Being a man is a matter of choice," it becomes obvious that a lot of men are making the wrong choices these days! There are a lot of boys who need to grow up and mature into manhood. Dr. Cole also says, "When a man acts like a child, he forces his wife to act like his mother." No real man wants to be married to his mother.

When Adam and Eve sinned, God did not call out to Eve. *God was looking for a man.* "Adam, where are you?" Adam was hiding because he knew he had sinned. He knew he should have stepped forward and said, "No, devil, we will not eat from this tree. The Lord rebuke you." Adam kept silent instead, and his descendants are still eating the fruits of his sin!

In the Family

Choices lead to responsibilities. I remember something my dad said one time while Gina and I were getting ready for our wedding day. Gina had some large boxes delivered to the house to be stored, and she asked me to take a big box from one end of the house to the other. My dad heard me grunting my way down the hall and came out of his room. It was a little warm and sweat was just rolling down. Dad started laughing at me as he bent down to help me put the thing in a closet. He said, "This is the way it's going to be from now on, son! Let me help you, man, but get used to it!"

That man followed me all the way to the other side of the house, laughing at me the whole time. Then he fell down on the ground just so he could laugh a little harder! I'll never forget what he said next between his tears of laughter: "Now you're going to find out *what it means to be a real man!* To be a *real responsible person.*" The commitment to marriage is a lifetime commitment to responsibility and true manhood. My father knew that, and I'm learning more about it every day. It is easy to preach and pray, and even to minister to thousands of people—but what about taking out the trash at home? How do you handle the clash between divine purpose and practical responsibility?

Most abuse and neglect in the Christian world comes from our failure to handle this conflict between calling and commitment. God demands that we meet both, but we have to do it His way.

I heard a preacher say one time, "When I'm in ministry, I'm not a father. I'm not a husband." I had to think about that statement. Later I asked my wife, "How would you like it if I said that?" Gina said without hesitation, "I wouldn't like it." There has never been a time when I have *not been a father* since my baby boy was born. There has never been a time when I *have not been Gina's husband* since we were married. I don't care how high or heavy my anointing is, or how busy I may become, I have made covenant commitments to my family before God. I told my preacher friend, "We have to be careful about saying those kind of things, because we send the wrong signal."

I don't want my little boy, Julian, to ever think that God took me away from him. I don't want Julian to ever have to say he had to step aside while "God and my father went away." I don't want him to ever feel that God invaded his life to destroy it, and leave him and his mama alone! I told Gina, "When I'm gone, help Julian respect what is happening, so he will feel honored and happy. If you're sad, and he's sad, then it is a bad experience. Make him feel good about it." When I'm gone, Gina tells our son, "Papa is gone in the work of the Lord, but he'll be back. We will pray for him while he's gone, that he'll have a speedy return."

The life of Moses seems to be a continuous string of one outstanding miracle after another, yet he failed in one of the most important areas of life. It took the bold intervention of his father-in-law to bring balance to his life.

How could Moses fulfill his divine destiny to deliver two million Israelites out of 400 years of enslavement and still be a decent husband? Was it necessary or even right for Moses to send away his wife and children to live with her father? I don't think it is *ever* right to send your wife and children away (except for brief periods in times of physical danger or logistical expediency).

Evidently Jethro, the father-in-law of Moses, felt that "enough was enough." He sent word ahead to Moses that he was coming to meet him, along with the wife and children he had sent away. Here you have a man of divine purpose, ministering under the anointing and flowing in his divine calling, but being forced to face his failure to recognize and fulfill his earthly responsibility as a husband and father.

We don't know what Moses was thinking when Jethro arrived with the family, but Moses went out to meet his father-in-law, bowed down, and kissed him (see Ex. 18:6-7). This was the only strong male image that Moses had in his life. You don't ever hear about his father—just his mother, his sister, the Egyptian princess who found him in the reeds and adopted him, and his wife, Zipporah.

Moses told his father-in-law all about the miracles God had done to deliver Israel, and Jethro said, "Praise be to the Lord, who rescued you from the hand of the Egyptians" (Ex. 18:10). He recognized the destiny and divine call on his son-in-law, but he had returned with Moses' wife and children nonetheless. He was publicly reminding Moses that he had a covenant obligation to honor—divine calling or not.

The next day, Moses went to work as usual. He didn't take a day off, even though his family had come in from out of town. When Jethro saw all that Moses was doing for the people, he asked, "What is this you are doing for the people? Why do you alone sit as judge, while all these people stand around you from morning till evening?" (Ex. 18:14b) When Moses basically answered the same way thousands of ministers have answered that question, "Well, the people *need me*," he was also saying, "I don't have time for my wife and children—I'm too busy doing the will of God by meeting the needs of the people." Question: Who's supposed to meet the needs of the family? Is God some divine substitute for His so-called anointed servants in their homes? I think not.

Neglect of family has never been part of God's will. Defaulting on a lifelong covenant commitment has never been His intention—in fact, these actions carry severe consequences throughout the Bible! Then Moses' father-in-law said something that no one else had the courage or authority to say: "What you are doing is *not good*. This is going to wear you out!" (see Ex. 18:17-18)

Sometimes we need wise "fathers" to speak into our lives and bring correction and balance. At Jethro's recommendation, Moses selected trusted men and trained them to help shoulder the day-to-day responsibilities of judging matters among the people. Jethro introduced Moses to the principle of delegation, mentoring, and management, and it saved his life, his ministry, and his marriage.

One time Gina, Julian, and I were visiting her family in Lake Charles, Louisiana. We were scheduled to fly to New Orleans for two days of meetings, and then she had to attend a women's conference for two days in Phoenix. On the plane from New Orleans to DFW, I asked Gina, "Sweetheart, why don't *I* take Julian on home with me so you can go on to

Phoenix without any encumbrance right now? That way you can give yourself to the meeting, enjoy yourself, and enjoy the ladies." Julian was about a year old and still nursing. She said, "Honey, are you serious?" I gave her my best little boy look and said, "Yes, baby, I am."

Gina looked at me and said, "Honey, that really speaks volumes to me." That caught me off guard. "What?" I asked. She just smiled and replied, "That you would take the baby." I told her, "Hey, I'm his father. God used me to bring him here, and God will use me to keep him here." I kept my word, and had one of the most memorable times of intimate bonding I have ever had with my son. (Yet the whole time, I was also thinking about the two services I had to preach Sunday morning in Tulsa, the Sunday night and Monday morning meetings in New Jersey, the Monday evening and two Tuesday services on Long Island, and the Wednesday flight to Buffalo to drop off 30 tons of food before taping a TV show, and the work to produce an Azusa conference I would face that Thursday and Friday!)

When Gina returned, she just couldn't stop kissing me and telling me how much she appreciated me.

What is precious to you? What do you cherish? In the midst of all the other things that you do, what is the dearest and nearest to your heart? I'm 43 years old now, and I'm thinking of what it means to me to get a hug and kiss from my mom. The other day, my dad came in and said, "Carlton, you're my Julian, you know." That almost made me cry. Even though I'm a pastor and a preacher, I still want to be somebody's "Julian," because I'm crazy about my own Julian.

Sometimes I don't want to be seen as a pastor, or an evangelist, or a preacher. Sometimes I want to be seen as a "Julian." I love it when my wife keeps kissing me and saying how much she appreciates me. I'm so glad that someone wants my touch. I'm so glad somebody likes to be close to me. I cherish people, because people count. You are important, and even your hurts and longings are important to God. While the devil is constantly shouting into our ears, "You're *naked—you're incomplete—you're not good enough*," God is saying something different.

The Virgin's Name Was Mary

In Luke 1:27, Scripture says, "The virgin's name was Mary." Mary, of course, was the name of our Lord's earthly mother, the betrothed wife of Joseph. The story is all too familiar to most Christians; however, I'd like to approach it from an angle that may be new to most readers. It's an interesting insight into the subject of self-image, self-worth, and whether or not we like ourselves.

The angel said to her, "Greetings, you who are highly favored! The Lord is with you" (Lk. 1:28). The King James Version says, "Blessed art thou among women." These are all very highly complimentary statements by the angel to this young teenaged woman betrothed to a man possibly several years her senior.

Verse 29 continues, "Mary was greatly troubled at his words and wondered what kind of greeting this might be," or what it might mean. Evidently she couldn't relate to those complimentary words. They didn't necessarily resonate with her spirit. The angel then tried to calm her by saying, "Do not be afraid, Mary, you are have found favor with God" (Lk. 1:30). The Greek word for "afraid" there would be phobia. He was saying, "Don't have a phobia about being favored by the Lord"!

Why did Mary have difficulty accepting the angel's compliments? Did she not feel favored of the Lord? Did she not feel that the Lord was with her? Did she not feel blessed among women, or in comparison to other women, or along with other women? Why was she troubled at these words? As I think about it, isn't that typical of many women who have difficulty receiving compliments? Tell a woman that her dress is beautiful and she'll say, "Oh, this old thing? I got it on sale." Tell her that her hair looks pretty and she might say, "Thank you, but I wish he had not cut it so short" or "The rinse is a little darker than I want it." Tell her she looks like she is losing weight and she'll say, "Oh, I could lose ten more pounds." Tell her that her nails are beautiful and she's liable to say, "Oh, they're really not mine"! Again, why is it so hard for many women to accept legitimate and worthy compliments?

Let's go back again to verse 27: "The virgin's name was Mary." The word *virgin* in Greek is the word *parthenos*. It means "to be untampered with, unviolated, kept secret, or of marital age." It comes from a Hebrew word that suggests to be hidden or kept out of sight. So you could say the hidden name or nature is Mary (the word *name* in the Greek means "character or nature"). The word *Mary* comes from the Hebrew name *Miriam*. It, in turn, is derived from the Hebrew word *Marah*, which means "bitterness, resentfulness, or even rebellion." Remember the bitter waters of Marah in Exodus 15:23.

Miriam was angry and bossy; she disdained playing second fiddle to Moses' Ethiopian wife (see Num. 12:1-9). So let's paraphrase the term again. Instead of saying "the virgin's name was Mary," perhaps the hidden meaning is "the hidden nature was bitterness, rebellion, or resentfulness."

Most people think the virgin Mary was the only perfect woman on the planet that God could find worthy of impregnating with the world's Redeemer, Jesus Christ. Another way to look at it however, which is just as reasonable, is to see Mary as a beautiful young woman on the outside, a good religious girl following the normal Jewish traditions of betrothal, commitment, and ultimately marriage, but maybe inside she was angry, hurt, and resentful both about herself and possibly about the elderly gentleman she was engaged to. Maybe God was using her as a symbol of the human race, or just the Jewish race—full of religious rituals but with no real inner joy or peace; not liking themselves, feeling unloved and unaccepted by God, and shocked by any possible suggestion that He might be pleased with them.

This could even go back to the empty feelings Eve had in the Garden of Eden after the Fall. When in the midst of that feeling of rejection by God because of their disobedience and rebellion, they rushed to cover up their own nakedness with leaves from a fig tree. Perhaps that was the beginning of women's tendency to go on wild shopping sprees, buying clothes in anxious and futile attempts to cover up something of which they are ashamed and afraid.

Praise God, Jesus comes to save and deliver us from the slavery and drudgery of low opinions of ourselves and all our self-worth problems, and to elevate us to the level of divine redemption, self-acceptance, and unconditional love.

Even today, millions of women every day put on tons of mascara (mask-ara), in many cases, in a subconscious desire to mask (cover up) facing who they really are or what they are afraid they really are. Unfortunately, this fear invades many of our relationships, both inner and extra personal, causing friction, dissonance, and conflicting disruptions. We need to learn how to accept the redeeming grace of God and love ourselves so we can love our neighbors likewise (see Lk. 10:27).

People Don't Like Themselves

Do you like yourself? Most people don't like themselves, let alone love themselves, as we just said. It does not have anything to do with the color of their skin or their sex. We spend millions of dollars as a society trying to improve ourselves by concentrating on the external with cosmetics, nails, clothes, weight, and tooth-brighteners, instead of working on the internal.

God asked Adam and Eve, "Who told you that you were naked?" (Gen. 3:11)

Today, God's question is just as relevant as the day He addressed it to Adam and Eve:

"Who told you that you were naked? What are you hiding from? Who told you that you were less than perfect? Who told you that you were less than I ordained you to be? Did you eat from the forbidden tree? Who convinced you to impress anyone but Me?"

Do you get so unhappy that you go shopping or go out to eat just to feel better?

Do you say, "I am depressed and lonely. I don't like me, so I'll buy a new jacket or a new pair of boots. That'll make people like me better. I'll get a bigger car—yes, and a nicer car. If I cannot afford that, then I'll just go get the biggest Big Mac I can find and at least make my belly feel better"?

Where did you get those questions and those answers? It wasn't from God. You will never please that critical voice inside that says:

"I'm too fat. I'm too black. I'm too white. I'm too skinny. I'm too tall. I'm too short. My hair isn't right. My nose isn't right. My lips aren't right. My feet are too big or too small. I don't fit. I'm not smart enough. I don't have enough money. I'm not educated enough. I don't know the right words or people. My clothes aren't good enough. Who am I? I'm different. I'm not of their denomination. I don't go to their upscale church. I'm not of the same race. I'm outnumbered. What is wrong with me?!" And on and on and on.

We need to stop hating ourselves. God says, "Love your neighbor as yourself" (Lev. 19:18). How are we ever going to love our neighbor *if we cannot even love ourselves?*

Relationships with others begin in our own hearts and minds. It is time to break from the painful failures and frustrations of the past and take hold of the future in Christ Jesus. It is no accident that God's Word declares to failure-prone human beings: "Therefore, if anyone is in Christ, he is a new creation; the old has gone, the new has come!" (2 Cor. 5:17)

Chapter 7

The Curse of Our Day

He will turn the hearts of the fathers to their children, and the hearts of the children to their fathers; or else I will come and strike the land with a curse (Malachi 4:6).

A curse has come upon our nation. We are losing our children to the streets, to drugs, and to gangs—mostly because fathers have ignored the precepts laid down in Scripture about raising a godly family!

However, before we point our finger at "the world" in righteous anger, think of the countless "born-again" fathers who only give lip service to God every Sunday morning, and never seek His way of teaching their children during the week.

The typical American father (whether he is a Christian or not) is disconnected from his family even when he is home! In his book, *Maximized Manhood*, Dr. Cole says the average American father only gives about 35 seconds of undivided attention to his child each day! He says the absentee father is "the curse of our day."[31]

Your sons and your daughters shall be given to another people, and your eyes shall look and fail with longing for them

all day long; and there shall be no strength in your hand
(Deuteronomy 28:32 NKJ).

God warned the Israelites under the Old Covenant that they would be cursed if they did not obey His voice and observe His commandments. One prominent Hebrew term for "curse" is *cherem*, which means "to be secluded or doomed; to be marked or designated for extermination or slaughter, to denounce or disdain or even disassociate."[32]

One of the most devastating of those curses was that parents would lose their children to other people—to captivity and bondage (to spirits, drugs, gangs, rebellion, etc.). In nearly every case, it was the actions of the people themselves that brought calamity upon their heads.

The average American father lounges back in his chair, drinks a six-pack of beer, and watches television on Sunday. If the telephone should ring on the end table right next to him, a little scenario takes place that is probably repeated in homes across America. While he is lounging, his wife is cooking, cleaning, changing diapers, or clearing off the table:

"Baby," he yells, "the phone's ringing!"

"Sweetheart, my hands are full. Can you answer it?"

He grumbles, but finally sets down his beer and picks up the phone. "Hello? Smith residence. Hang on a minute."

He puts his hand over the receiver and yells, "Hey, baby, it is the electric company." (It could also be the plumber, the school, the police, or even…"Hey, baby, God is on the phone!")

This is the picture of a man who has been *decapitated by satan*! He has abdicated his family responsibilities, even with his children, so he is living under the curse of the law. His unwillingness to accept responsibility taints every area of life in the home.

"Daddy, can I go outside?" his son asks. "Go ask your mama," the father answers.

"Daddy, can I have a sandwich?" The father answers, "Go ask your mama."

If a child said, "Daddy, can I breathe?" the absentminded answer would be, "Go ask your mama!" Eventually the child ceases to even consider his father when seeking permission, affirmation, or validation in his life.

When Daddy is consistently absent in body, mind, or spirit, he becomes *increasingly insignificant* in that family. The family learns to function without him.

The moment a father drops his guard and fails to watch over his family or accept his leadership responsibility, the enemy whacks off his head. One day he will rise from his easy chair to discover his children are running the streets, following after the god of this world (see 2 Cor. 4:4). He will not know them, and they will feel they no longer need or know him.

A Disobedient Nation

See, I will send you the prophet Elijah before that great and dreadful day of the Lord comes. He will turn the hearts of the fathers to their children, and the hearts of the children to their fathers; or else I will come and strike the land with a curse (Malachi 4:5-6).

The last two verses of Malachi chapter 4 display God's final Old Testament message to a disobedient nation. It was uttered 400 years before the birth of Jesus Christ.

Like Israel, America has become a disobedient nation. The spirits of King Ahab and Queen Jezebel are still active and are tearing our society apart! Today, as then, Ahab represents weak, indecisive, nonspiritual male leadership; and Jezebel, whose name means "unharnessed or unhusbanded," represents out-of-control female dominance and aggression.

We must turn the hearts of the fathers to their children once again. We must teach them how to be godly fathers so their children will not be forced to grow up in broken and divorced households filled with bitterness and distorted examples of married life. Children need a man's influence as well as that of a woman.

Death of a Dream

Brenda Reed's story is a perfect example of what I am saying. It appeared in an article printed in *USA Today* concerning black women who have watched their dreams die. Brenda's story echoes the pain of almost any single mother of any background, race, or culture who is struggling to survive.

"Growing up in Ohio, Brenda Reed dreamed of getting married and living in a house with a white picket fence, a husband, and two children. Now she sees those faded dreams as white ideals—a happily ever after, that, partly because of her own mistakes and partly because of a larger problem among blacks, was not destined to be hers. Never a white picket fence, two children, and a husband.

"At 37, Reed is twice divorced, a mother whose six children, like more than half of all black children in the USA, depend solely on her for their support. Last year, 51 percent of black children had no fathers in their home, a record high rate that has cultural and economic ramifications that could last for generations.

" 'Children in single-parent families are economically disadvantaged and that hurts their opportunities,' says Christine Moore, a sociologist of Child Trends, a Washington think tank. 'It makes it harder for black children to achieve economic mobility.'

"For Reed, single motherhood has meant watching her three sons drop out of high school one by one and feeling that only a father could have persuaded them to stay. It also has meant learning not to depend on men for financial or emotional security. If he is never there, you don't even think about him; you don't miss him.

" 'Black women are willing to take on the responsibility of a child because they believe they can do it,' says Reed, who now lives in Atlanta. 'But they do not want to take on the baggage of a man.' "[33]

Women are saying, "I can handle the children—I can handle their screams and their diapers—but I cannot handle this stupid, insensitive, distant, stoic, half-brained man who does not know I need his affection, his time, his attention, and his positive reinforcement. It causes too much pain. I'd rather raise these six children by myself. I do not like him. My daddy was not there, either."

That attitude is inspired by an insidious spirit that is spreading all over this land. Some experts say that this negative perspective is gaining prevalence as succeeding generations of black children grow up without fathers at home, but it is not only black children who are affected. The article continues:

"While the proportion of white children living in single-parent households has grown too, reaching 16 percent by 1990, the more dramatic increase has occurred among blacks. 'Part has to do with the culture and value systems within some segments of black populations,' says Timothy Brubaker, director of The Family and Child Studies center at Miami University in Ohio. 'Some black women do not expect black males to be involved as much because they have been in the situation of not having a father,' he said. 'The next generation sees only a mother. It is difficult to see another way.'

"Reed, a customer service representative for a health care company, is happier now than she was during either of her troubled marriages. But when she looks at her children, she worries they will repeat her mistakes. Reed dropped out of school at the tenth grade when she became pregnant. She has an equivalency degree but hasn't finished college. The oldest son, Kenneth, 19, says he just did not believe school would make a difference, looking around at better dressed white classmates. 'I just felt I was black and no matter what, I would fail.' "[34]

Being black is not an excuse for failing! Not having decent clothes is not an excuse for failing. It is time for all of us, especially people of color, to stop blaming our failure on the color of our skin or the size of our bank account.

That article concluded by saying:

"After fruitless struggles to control her oldest son, Reed eventually kicked him out of the house. He stayed with friends, in hotels, and on the street. Two weeks ago, he came home still looking for work, often being rejected. 'It seemed my life was doing nothing but going in a dumb, dead cycle.' But now Kenneth is in a pivotal position. His girlfriend is pregnant—potentially another black, single mother."[35]

We Have to Make a Change

In 1970, 58 percent of all black children lived with both parents. In 1990, only 37 percent came home to both parents in the same house. The problem goes far beyond the "color line." This pattern of serious family decline is not just affecting black or ethnic homes. It is invading all homes!

We have to make a change.

We have to take marriage seriously.

We need to understand that marriage should be a lifelong commitment.

We can only make that change with God's help.

The wedding is a celebration, but marriage is serious business. Once a bride takes off the long white wedding gown, she will never wear it again. Gina and I have not even thought about going back to pick up her wedding dress. We spent a lot of money on it because we wanted it to be beautiful, but now it is not that important. The wedding celebration is over. We still have fun, but marriage is more serious.

Myles Munroe has said, "If weddings are public, they ought to make it a law that divorce has to be public too!"

In our society, those who get married with great fanfare get divorced quietly. It is a joke. The very fabric of our society is being ripped apart by divorce, like a bridal gown that is left in the corner, discarded and torn.

The biggest share of the blame and the responsibility for change falls on men. Men need to assume their rightful place as husbands and fathers again. Our nation's future literally depends on it! Not all the blame, but most of the responsibility, falls to men.

Chapter 8

Talk Is Worth
Its Weight in Gold

A gentle answer turns away wrath, but a harsh word stirs up anger (Proverbs 15:1).

Americans spend more time trying to invent a better divorce than making a better marriage! We often say, "Talk is cheap"; however, between husband and wife, the right kind of talk is worth its weight in gold.

Conversation...communication...talking openly and honestly...all can save a marriage, save families, and save the future lives of children.

We put more planning and thought into how to split up the children and property than we do searching for solutions to save our marriages. We need to learn to talk to one another if we want to reverse the trend of absentee men in the home. Communication between a husband and wife is essential if the two are to remain one!

First, we need to find out who we are and accept who we are. Then we need to stop pretending to be someone we are not! It is time for us to be honest—even if it hurts. If you cannot accept yourself, then you cannot truly accept anyone else. Your discontent with yourself will be projected onto whoever you are intimate with. The "splinter" in that person's eye becomes magnified into a two-by-four!

Some of us think our haircuts are too short, and the rest of us think they are too long, that our hair is getting too thin, or that it's too gray (and I have not even brought up the touchy subject of baldness yet)! Whether your shoulders are broad or narrow, whether you are articulate like David, or slow of speech like Moses, it is time to accept yourself as God made you without apology, and let Him fulfill His purpose through you.

Perhaps you think your wife speaks a little better than you do, and you are bothered by the thought that she works with people (especially men) who are a little brighter, a little more educated, or a little "classier" than you are.

You may even know of a guy at her office or even at church who is "intellectually stimulating" to her (and you don't feel as if you can compete in that area). Listen, it will not matter how much brains another man has if you value your wife as a person and really listen to her when she talks!

Why did Adam neglect Eve?

Yes, I am assuming the first man neglected the first woman...and for the same reason we do it today: Adam failed to live with his wife "according to knowledge" (1 Pet. 3:7 KJV).

Why did he leave Eve lacking so much that she started fooling around with the guy wearing the "snake-skinned britches"?

Did Adam not notice that "slick-talkin' snake" was spending more time with Eve than he was?

Did the serpent affirm Eve in ways that Adam should have, but never did?

Did he ever give the excuse we use so much today: "I was too busy doing 'the work of the Lord'?"

That sharp-looking single serpent began to minister to Eve with beguiling whispers of "where, why, and what if...." Pssst...pssst...pssst. (*Nachash*, the Hebrew word for "serpent," literally means "to hiss or repeat an incantation.")

I can almost hear the tempter's carefully crafted words used in his first conquest of the human race—a devilish incantation framed to sound like genuine concern and compassion with Eve's "self-interest" at heart. I think that conversation probably sounded like millions of others that have taken place since then:

"Are you alone again?" the serpent hissed. "So your husband is still at work? Now just when does he come home?"

"Oh, he's probably off walking and talking with God somewhere in the cool of the day," Eve said. "He'll be home late this afternoon."

"You mean you have been here all day—all by yourself?"

"Yeah," Eve sighed.

"So you are stuck here with the animals every day by yourself?"

"Yeah. I get kind of lonely" (said this time with the first hint of a sniffle).

"Well, I am sure you do, you poor thing," satan hisses, crawling closer. "Do you always 'not dress' like that? I love what you are not wearing!" (said with a disapproving raised eyebrow—if he had one). "Boy, your man goes all out on your wardrobe, doesn't he?" he says with sinister sarcasm. "Humph!"

"The Snake Made Me Feel Great"

Satan was able to get to Eve because he was able to distort her relationship with Adam and with God. He made her feel important. A wife needs to know she is cherished. The silent treatment will not cut it. You have to tell a woman you love her, not just when you ask her to marry you, but every day and in every way until "death do you part." She craves that security of attention. Accept it, brothers—women are "high maintenance" partners.

Men tend to look at marriage as a contract that is signed one time. They squeeze out the words "I do" and "sign the dotted line" of commitment on the wedding day, so it is a done deal legally.

A woman knows better. Love thrives on personal investment and daily attention. She looks at words of love in the same way we husbands look at food, water, and sleep. We need generous amounts of all of these several times a day, every day, or something will suffer and breakdown eventually!

The moment satan offered Eve that forbidden fruit, Adam should have risen up and taken authority over him.

He should have said, "Wait a minute, honey. We don't need that! We have our love for each other, and God loves us. We don't need anything else." But he didn't. Or perhaps Adam's love and innocence made him timid and nonconfrontational. Perhaps he had been meaning to discuss the matter with Eve at some point, but had been procrastinating as some men tend to do.

In Hebrew, the words for "evil"—*ra*—and "shepherd"—*raah*—are very similar. A shepherd "attends" to his sheep. The peculiar danger of the serpent then (and now) was his subtle ability and crafty knack of attending to Eve's basic emotional needs.

It is possible that the hissing serpent in the garden became a more intimate friend to Eve than Adam was! If that sounds sad, it is because it is! Sadder still is the fact that many, if not most men, still neglect the basic relational needs of their wives. God has a better way if you and I will only listen!

If Adam had taken his rightful place as the spiritual head of his family, he would have drop-kicked the devil out of the garden and the "Fall" would not have happened! I am going to be blunt: It was Adam's responsibility and God-ordained assignment to protect his wife and rule the earth God gave him. When he didn't, someone else stepped up to do the job.

Eve looked for fulfillment and affirmation in someone or something else, and a slick-talkin' dude in snake-skinned boots stepped up to fill the void with soft enchantments of affirmation and illegal desires.

What about you? Is your neglect setting the stage for a new dude to take your place in your wife's life? Do not fall for the lie that this is something new or unique to you—this vicious cycle of neglect, which leads to fulfillment of forbidden desires, has been handed down from one generation to another since Adam and Eve! Now, that does not make it right; it simply shows us up as awfully slow learners.

Adam toiled and worked. Eve desired relationship. Males communicate to solve a problem, while females communicate for relationship. It is their way of getting closer, of developing intimacy with another person.

Neither pattern is wrong. Adam and Eve were each fulfilling their destiny. The problem is that they failed to build a bridge of "understanding relationship" to bond their two natures together as God meant them to be.

How many wives turn to their husbands and say, "Where are you? We don't spend enough time together. We never talk. We never really communicate. What time are you coming home? Why are you leaving? Where are you going? When is your day off? When do we have a vacation? We need more time together." Remember, God said to Eve (the woman), "Your desire will be for your husband" (Gen. 3:16).

Does that sound familiar? These questions are usually only "starter questions" that launch a sad and painful exchange of "non-communication" that goes like this:

"You never talk to me," the wife says.

"What do you want to talk about?" the husband grunts.

"I just want to talk," she says again.

When he ignores her and keeps reading the paper, her temperature rises and finally she says in "that voice" every married man knows so well: "Why don't you put down that stupid paper and look at me? And get your filthy feet off the coffee table. This isn't a barn!"

"Why don't you stop telling me what to do! I'm not your little boy," the surprised and wounded male responds in quick self-defense.

"Because I am the one who is expected to keep everything clean around here," she screams (all the while wishing they were talking in gentle tones about the longings of her heart). "I am not your slave, you know. I am not your mama, and I am surely not your maid!"

"Don't you yell at me, woman!" he yells (while he's really thinking, *Well, you sure sound like my mama—and I always did hate the sound of that tone of voice ordering me around*).

"I'll yell if I want to!" (This is sometimes followed by the full name of the accused with all applicable middle initials.) By this time, all the kids are hiding in their rooms, the next-door neighbors have turned down their TVs, and the folks at the retirement home on the corner have turned up their hearing aids so they will not miss any action!

"I am sick of you expecting me to pick up after you. I am sick of these kids, and I am sick of this cooking and cleaning! Every time I turn around, you are leaving your shoes in the middle of the floor!"

"Shut up, woman. If you were my maid, I'd fire you! You better start picking things up around here. I work hard all day and come home to a dirty house and dishes in the sink. What do you do all day, anyway?"

The man started it all by failing to live with his wife "according to knowledge," as the apostle Peter wrote:

Likewise, ye husbands, dwell with them according to knowledge, giving honour unto the wife, as unto the weaker vessel, and as being heirs together of the grace of life; that your prayers be not hindered (1 Peter 3:7 KJV).

The whole explosion could have been avoided with five minutes of personal, focused attention on his wife. Instead he kept his nose buried under a 75-cent newspaper and bought himself a big dose of grief and heartburn.

The woman is not guilt-free in this free-for-all either. She did the worst thing she could do: She reminded her husband of his mother.

"What is so bad about that?" you ask.

She did not remind her mate of the "warm fuzzy" part of Mom. She resurrected all the memories buried in his subconscious about being a "helpless and dependent little boy" getting a "tongue-lashing." No man on earth responds well in that situation. It deflates his ego and wounds his pride, so he will instantly lash out at whoever is doing it, now that he is grown up and "does not have to take it any longer." It doesn't matter how spirit-filled a man is; he still has to deal (wrestle) with his masculine pride and ego.

Since marriages do not exist in vacuums, any explosion engulfs every breathing being within those four walls. The dog gets booted out the door, the cat gets swatted, and both parents look for the nearest kid to blame and dispatch with an order to "pick up the house."

After nearly every fight, spouses like to get "legalistic" and carefully divide their duties. Mama quits disciplining the kids for a day or two, and "saves" it for Dad to do.

What kid has not heard these words before: "You just wait till your Dad gets home!"

You have one guess as to the first thing Dad gets to do when he walks in the door—discipline his children. And, because he is tired from the day and aggravated at his wife for doing this to him, he probably will be too harsh on his children, or he might ignore them altogether.

Thus he will "provoke" them to anger (KJV)—which the apostle Paul admonished fathers not to do in two different letters—and so plants "seeds" of bitterness in them that will affect the lives of their own families later. The New International Version says:

Fathers, do not exasperate your children; instead, bring them up in the training and instruction of the Lord (Ephesians 6:4).

Fathers, do not embitter your children, or they will become discouraged (Colossians 3:21).

Paul also wrote for husbands not to be "harsh" with their wives (Col. 3:19). Generally a man gets harsh and brutish when he feels cornered or captured by threatening circumstances. That's when he must control himself before he tries to control anybody else—especially his wife and children.

The Doormat Wife

Although some wives can give as much fight as they get, others were born (or raised) with a different personality. They are not the type to fight back. This kind of wife may have a sweeter spirit, or perhaps she has been so abused in the past that she has no self-esteem and rather has a "victim" spirit. One harsh word from her husband may crush her spirit, sometimes irreparably.

Careless or unthinking men can devastate women in unintentional ways such as this:

"What do you need at the store, baby?" the husband asks. (He wants a big bag of potato chips and a two-liter bottle of soda, so he thinks he will do her a big favor by picking up a gallon of milk at the same time.)

"Oh, nothing," she smiles. "The kids are in bed. Let's just sit and talk for awhile."

The husband knows good and well there is no milk for his cereal in the morning. He frowns at her while wondering, *Did she wreck the car or something?*

"What would we talk about?" he asks (while thinking, *Maybe I forgot to do something she asked me to do*).

"I just want to talk."

"Be more specific."

"Well, you know, nothing specific."

"Sweetheart," he growls, "I don't have time to talk about nothing! The world could come to an end while we are talking about nothing! Jesus is probably coming back the day after tomorrow, and I have bills to pay tonight—and you want to talk about nothing. Now what do you want at the store?"

What message does this man's wife get from a conversation like this?

He is saying, "You are not important—groceries are more important."

She feels worthless. While he goes to the store for his precious potato chips and soda pop, his wife lays across the bed, crying her eyes out. A woman needs relationship. She needs to be able to talk to her husband, even when he cannot see any reason for it.

I know it's difficult, but we husbands must "give up" ourselves for our wives (Eph. 5:25). It's demanding, it's restrictive, and it's obligatory—but it is also an absolute necessity in order to keep our homes steady and on course.

The Mothering Wife

I think wives get confused sometimes because their husbands seem to send "mixed signals." When a man is sick, he wants his wife to come in and "mother" him, nurture him, and love him back to health. But think about the examples already given.

I experienced this myself. Six months into our marriage, I had to have rotator cuff surgery and it left me without the normal use of my right arm for months. During that time I had to depend on my wife in ways I hadn't even considered before we were married.

Just a year earlier my parents had moved in with me to help take care of my 84-year-old grandfather, who was a widower and took turns staying with his grandchildren. Strangely enough, I loved having my parents in my home—especially the special attention I received from my mother.

As I look back, I see now how I compared Gina's care of me to what I knew my mother would do. I expected my wife to suddenly become "Supermom" for me. Under those circumstances, I cherished a "matriarchal wife." However, in most normal situations I would have found the motherly antics irritating and unacceptable.

As soon as Gina asks me, "Did you take out the trash?" the picture suddenly changes and the rebellious spirit manifests. The male ego rises up and demands honor and respect. We men must be careful of the signals we send to our wives, and wives need to be sensitive to men's paranoia in that area.

Who's in the House?

If a man feels insignificant at home, he may spend more time outside the home, even on the job, because that is where his ego is stroked more. This should not be a mystery to anyone who stops to think about it.

At work, the husband may be "the boss." He may have a secretary. I can almost guarantee you that, if so, his secretary wears beautiful clothes and sweet-smelling perfume, and brings his coffee exactly as he likes it. She also protects him from people he does not want to see. This secretary doesn't necessarily do this for personal reasons, because she is "after a man" or after him, but because she is a professional. Secretaries who don't smell pleasantly or who fail to assist their bosses usually do not last long.

His secretary encourages him, saying things like, "We can do it, boss. You are going to come out on top." It may shock you, but she "ministers to" or serves him. She's usually sensitive to his ego needs and knows how and when to stroke that ego. She gives him her loyalty and support. In other words, she nurtures him.

Meanwhile, what if all the man can remember about his wife is how she sounded like his mother that morning? That she seemed to be in opposition to or insensitive to the concerns he has on the job?

What if the "tape" of the morning's conversation runs through his memory all day? When he goes home that evening, he has spent a day with hectoring questions like these running through his mind over and over:

"What time are you coming home tonight? Don't forget to go by the cleaners and pick up your shirts. And don't forget to pick up a loaf of bread at the store. Are you wearing the same underwear again? Did you fix the lock on the bathroom door?" And so forth, on and on.

As the secretary hands him a second cup of coffee, he may think of what he will face when he gets home.

He knows his wife will say, "Did you go by the cleaners?"

Since he often forgets to do the errands assigned last night or in the predawn hours, he will have to say, "No, baby, I forgot. But I'll do it tomorrow." He feels like a disobedient child being interrogated. There's nothing sexy or romantic about that feeling whatsoever.

But all day at the office, his secretary is saying, "Yes, sir. What do you need, sir? Right away, sir. Yes, sir, I'll take care of it for you. Do not worry about a thing. That is what I am here for."

I am not saying a woman's reason for existence is to make life rosy for men, or that we ought not to have to worry about anything. I am not talking so much about behavior as about communication.

If a wife can understand why her husband reacts the way he does, she can "tone down" her requests and reminders. A husband will find his wife's approach to him much sweeter if he understands that she will "tone down" her voice and attitude when he gives her the same quality time and attention he would to a customer or a client. She needs her time and attention from him, and he needs his space and place beyond.

The "Right to Rip" Clause

No one would speak to someone else like a spouse does to the husband or wife! Perhaps she feels that since she married him, she has a license to "rip" into him. Anyone else would get fired or "punched." Husbands speak to their wives in ways they would not speak to anyone else. Some witless husbands yell at their wives as they would at a stray dog, shouting, "You can't do anything right!"

When you know someone well, you have the power to cut him or her to the quick. Your intimate knowledge of that person's weaknesses, fears, insecurities, and personal failings (and we all have them) helps you know what to say and how to say it in a way that causes the most hurt or damage!

The beauty of the godly marriage is that love is to cover this multitude of sins and shortcomings.

The curse of the ungodly marriage is that spite and selfishness will uncover and ridicule every hidden hurt and fear! Unfortunately, even Christian marriage partners are exploiting one another's needs instead of meeting them.

A Balance Between Head and Heart

Most men hide their emotions well. They are trained from infancy not to laugh or cry easily. We do not respond as quickly or as readily as women, but we do think. We tend to favor our logical side, because it makes life more predictable. We prefer to ponder and use reason. We analyze and question. But sometimes logic can trip us up. We want things to "make sense" when logical analysis is not always what is needed.

We get trapped in our heads, and some of the really important things in life never filter down to our hearts. We don't really know what is in our hearts because our heads speak so loudly. Men need to get into balance. We need to recognize and value the feminine aspect of our nature. There is a more tender, lenient, and pliable side of us that God placed in us for a reason. We must get in touch with that side of us in order to better understand our wives or even women at large—mothers, sisters, and friends.

Too many men have been conditioned by culture and/or society to hide any "meekness" in their natures. Listen, *meekness does not mean weakness*! Jesus said the "meek" will inherit the earth (Mt. 5:5)! Meekness in the biblical sense means "teachableness."

We are called by God to be kind and gentle, yet strong, forceful, and decisive! We need to bring true masculine leadership and direction into our homes, while speaking kindly and respectfully to our wives so that our prayers will be answered (see 1 Pet. 3:7)!

Let me start meddling a little bit: Husbands, you need to love your wives even when they don't respect you! Wives, you need to *respect* and honor your husbands even when they do not seem to cherish you. There is a reason the apostle Paul wrote for husbands to "love" their wives and wives to "respect" their husbands (see Eph. 5:25,33).

Love causes women to respect and honor those who love them.

Respect for a husband's headship brings the household into God's order and allows prayers to be answered. If you cannot yet respect the man himself because he is a sinner or has unsanctified ways, you can at least respect the office of husband and be tolerant of the man's defects and shortcomings in light of God's Word.

We may not like a certain President of the United States. We may not agree with everything he does. But we can respect the office he holds and treat him with respect because of the solemnity of that office. Every office of headship or authority demands respect because the person in that office is a "stand-in" for Jesus.

All authority is ordained by God to bring order into society and our lives (see Rom. 13:1-2), even if it doesn't appear that God has placed that particular person there. In America, our right to choose whom we want in office is respected by God. However, once they are in office, their hearts are in *His* hands (see Prov. 21:1).

Wives, even if God did not choose the husband you have, even if you did your own picking, once you are married, he is in the office of headship, which is God's office. Honor that office, if you want to prosper. God will honor it too. (read First Corinthians 7:12-14.)

Husbands, Jesus loved you while you were unlovable—and now it is your turn to love your wives, whether or not they are lovable. It is the price of leadership, the price of holding a headship office.

We need to dwell with our wives "with understanding." They may not be accustomed to submitting to men. Perhaps they were reared without a father. Or perhaps there is a "root of bitterness" present at their brothers, because of physical or even mental abuse suffered at their hands. Either way, we must be prayerfully and lovingly patient and tolerant of what we may not agree with.

We have already established that women in general enjoy talking more than most men do. Women have a broader command of the language than most men and, even from infancy, begin speaking much earlier than their male counterparts.

I discovered early in my marriage that when a woman speaks, she is generally saying what she feels. She speaks out of her emotions and deeper sentiment. When men speak, we are usually saying what we think; we feel comfortable communicating from an almost exclusively analytical, or logical, viewpoint. We often notice how our wives can frequently and quickly succumb to tears while trying to voice their feelings.

The husband will say, "Gosh, sweetheart. Can't we just talk this out without your crying? Come on, honey, what are you crying about?"

She is crying because she is "feeling," or because she is frustrated in trying to express her feelings. Remember, she is relationship-oriented and experiences considerably more deep sentiment than the average man.

I not only had to learn to listen for what my wife was saying, but also to probe, discern, and discover what she was actually communicating behind, or in addition to, the tears and emotion. That is where communication begins.

Most of us men are married to our visions, our passions, and our careers. We need to ask our wives to forgive us for neglecting them. We need to ask their forgiveness for accusing them, judging them, and being harsh.

Have you looked at life from her viewpoint? Perhaps she is impatient and frustrated because she is tired of you sitting in front of the tube like a zombie, watching back-to-back football games until your eyes glaze over, but not spending quality time with her.

Someone needs to bring order to our crippled society—and God says the buck stops with *the man in the house*!

Chapter 9

You Can
Understand Your Wife

Do not be deceived: God cannot be mocked. A man reaps what he sows. The one who sows to please his sinful nature, from that nature will reap destruction; the one who sows to please the Spirit, from the Spirit will reap eternal life (Galatians 6:7-8).

Most men hear statements that "put women down" while they are growing up. Eventually they say the same things to their sons without thinking where they got them. They simply repeat them as if they are "the gospel truth." If we tell our sons such things, they in turn will tell their sons the same, and false generalities about the opposite sex will go on down through the generations causing trouble. Future generations will reap what we have sown, just as we are reaping what Adam and Eve sowed.

These things are such clichés as:

You will never understand a woman, so do not even try!
There comes a time when a woman will get in a mood.

Just ignore her. Shut her off, shut her down, leave her alone. She is crazy!

Men, we must stop that! You need to understand that when you say those things about your wife, you cut her off from yourself spiritually! You leave her out in a dangerous place all by herself. Men do not adequately understand a woman's nature or her hormonal systems. We do not know what she is going through, but worst of all, *we do not try to know*!

We have been brainwashed to believe that we don't have to understand our wives because our dads didn't understand our mothers! *Sometimes we act like God probably doesn't really understand a woman either!*

The truth is that if a man would take the time to cultivate a relationship with a woman, it would bear a hundredfold harvest! Women are responders because God made them that way. A woman responds to a man's overtures by giving her whole heart to him—*all they need to know is that they are appreciated.*

Remember, the enemy wants to distort every relationship between a man and a woman, and he will use whatever method he thinks will work. He tries to distort and twist our thinking about one another to get us off balance. Why?

According to Genesis, as we have noticed, there came a time in the creation process when God stopped saying, "It is good," and said something was "bad," or incomplete and unfinished (see Gen. 2:18).

Satan probably already was lurking around trying to spy out what God was doing and what He meant by it. When he heard God say, "It is not good," his so-called pointed ears must have perked up.

"What is not good?" he thought. "I wonder what is not good?"

As he continued to listen, he heard God muse aloud, "It is not good that man should be alone in history, just man and the animals. Man needs someone like himself. Man cannot extend himself without a female. Without woman, man becomes extinct. It is not good that man should live a solitary existence."

"Ah ha," the devil must have thought. "Now I know what is not good on the earth."

From that day to this, satan has spent much of his time trying to keep men and women apart in heart and body, except for the purposes of sin and destruction. His primary objective is to destroy God's creation and satisfy his lust for revenge and hateful spite. If he cannot destroy mankind with homosexuality, he will try to build a wall between husbands and wives.

Some people can actually live together for 30 or 40 years and *still* not know or even like one another! They are just enduring the relationship. They stay together "for the sake of the kids."

I heard a funny story illustrating this: One couple had been married almost 80 years. When he was 100, and she was 98, the husband decided he was going to divorce his wife!

Someone asked, "You've been together so long—after all these years, why on earth would you want a divorce?"

They answered, "We wanted to stay together *until all the kids died.*"

Children are one of many good reasons to stay together, but they should not be the primary reason. Love and respect are the main reasons you should work on your marriage.

A Walk on the Wild Side

I can almost imagine the serpent sitting around in the garden of Eden thinking to himself, "How can I separate Adam and Eve?"

Then he hit on a plan. He would distort Eve's image of who she really was. Satan seduced Eve into experimenting with good and evil. When you've always lived a good life, there is a strong temptation to experiment with evil.

One friend of mine grew up in a very strict Holiness church. He told me he went to Oral Roberts University in Tulsa, Oklahoma, just to get away from his hometown! He said he attended a movie theater 21 times in a row just to see the same movie. Why? It was the first time he had ever been allowed to go to a movie in his life. He was fascinated by it, because he had been told it was *forbidden fruit*!

In my ministry, I have found that many people who were brought up in very strict, religious, legalistic backgrounds go "hog-wild" when they finally escape, and they "backslide" as fast as possible. It seems they do things that even the devil has not thought of doing! They are like a dog that has been cooped up in a house all day. The second you let him out, he goes crazy and runs all over the place! Sometimes, in his excitement, he runs into the street and right in front of a speeding car.

What is it in the human spirit that makes us want to go wild? It is the rebellion, self-will, and pride that rose up in the spirits of mankind when Adam and Eve sinned and lost the life of God within themselves. It is the "adamic" human nature, which is always opposed to the things of God.

You may say, "But, Brother Carlton, there are a lot of other children who were brought up in the same church system who never rebel to such extremes."

You are right, I am one of them; but most of them live joyless lives. Most of the ones I have ministered to suffered because their personalities have been distorted by the incorrect image of a God just waiting to pounce on them if they did something wrong. They basically dislike themselves, and are always striving to be perfect so that somehow they can win God's approval—as well as man's.

Some people with strong (outward) "holiness" backgrounds have such a bad perception of sex that it spills over into their marriages. In their minds, sex is such a dirty, ungodly, and sinful act that they cannot give themselves sexually to their mates in holy matrimony without feeling as if they have committed a terrible sin!

Many of the girls who were brought up in the Pentecostal church with me had to wear long dresses, and their blouses had to be buttoned all the way up their necks. They could not cut their hair, tint it, or put a permanent in it. This "programs" into girls' minds that the body itself is somehow not good or nice.

When a spirit of religion comes into a marriage, it can kill the relationship! It excises every hint of romantic love and passion, and causes both partners to do everything in a mechanical way. The husband and wife go through decades of a dull marriage "doing their marital duties," never realizing that all the joy and passion displayed in the Song of Solomon is ours to enjoy in the marriage bed! There is no love in these bound-up religious unions—only obligation.

We do not need obligation. We need inspiration!

The serpent has skillfully perverted the sexual union of a man and woman. He has done his best to rob us of God's best for our marriages by making sex seem ugly or dirty. Legalism can cripple you for life once it gets a grip on your mind.

Some of the kids I knew who came from strict religious systems were helpless in real life! Watching their lives was like watching a dog that had spent most of its life on a short leash. Year after year, that dog learned it could run only as far as the leash allowed it to run. Every time it hit the end of the leash, the dog was pulled up short. After a while, it was trained to run only so far.

When the leash was removed, the dog still refused to go farther than the spot where he had been pulled up short so many times! Animal trainers have learned that, even if all food or water is placed just outside that old stopping place, the dog will die of thirst or starvation *before it will cross that programmed line*! The truth is that *a lot of us are crippled because we've learned psychologically that we can only go so far in life*. We have a poor self-image. We have been programmed for limitation and mediocrity.

Do You Have a Poor Self-Image?

If you are experiencing difficulties in a relationship right now, it is almost certain that they are caused in whole or in part by your poor self-image, the poor self-image of the other person, or both. If you are not happy or secure with yourself, you will project that unhappiness onto someone else. You will not be comfortable with the differences between the two of you.

For instance, could I be as comfortable in my wife's Toyota Camry as I am in my Cadillac? No, I do not even want to be as comfortable in it. *But I should be.* What do I feel when I am in my Cadillac that I do not feel in her Camry (besides the leather seats)? What does a Cadillac, or a Mercedes, or a Lexus do for my male ego? Why do I feel better in ostrich-skin boots? If I wear tennis shoes, does that change my self-worth? Does that change who I am? *Of course not.* Will it make my wife or other people love me less? It shouldn't.

The enemy will try to distort your self-worth and self-image by using external things. Sinbad the comedian has told this story of a good-looking single man who was well-known on the party circuit:

> "He dressed sharply, and when he went to a party, he had the 'pick' of the ladies [obviously he wasn't a Christian...]. He seemed to have it all together—until he finally got married and disappeared from the party scene for six or eight months.

> "Finally, someone saw him in a mall walking behind his wife carrying her purse, almost as if he had become brain damaged! Before he got married, he was smart, happy-go-lucky, and dressed as sharply as he wanted. Once he got married, it was a different story.

> "Several years later, he and his wife decided to go out one night, and he came in all dressed up in one of the outfits he used to wear as a single guy. His wife took one look at him and said, 'I know you're not wearing that! You know that stuff doesn't match.'

> " 'What is the matter with what I have on, baby?' he asked. 'Oh, honey,' she said, shaking her head. 'You're not wearing that.'

> " 'Well, what do you want me to wear, honey?' She had trained him real well by now. 'Go in there and sit down. After I get ready, I'll dress you.' So this grown man sits down on the bed next to his little son. While both of them are waiting to be dressed, the former swinger says to his boy, 'Son, Mama's going to dress us in a little while. I sure hope she lets me wear my new shirt I got for Christmas!' " (The place roars with laughter.)

We laugh, but it happens. We are always trying to change our mates and family members into our own image. We are not comfortable allowing them to develop in the image of God. A browbeaten man will either knuckle under and hate himself and possibly his wife, or he will escape back to his single lifestyle, leaving behind a fatherless son and a bitter, angry woman. I remember hearing my mother say while teaching a group of ladies in our church " 'I do' does not mean I re-do."

Restless Vagabonds

And Adam knew Eve as his wife, and she became pregnant and bore Cain; and she said, I have gotten and gained a man with the help of the Lord (Genesis 4:1 AMP).

With the help of the Lord, Eve gained a man. Did she not already have "a man" before in her husband? It appears here that although Eve had a husband, she saw Cain as "her own man," her personal possession. She had her own *ish*, her own male person!

According to *Strong's Concordance*, Cain's name means "spear." It is derived from the Hebrew word *coon*, which means "to chant or wail (at a funeral)."[36] Eve named her son "Ca-in" because she lamented and wailed during his birth. God warned her she would experience increased pain in childbirth as a result of sin. It was not His original plan, but Adam and Eve's disobedience brought pain and sorrow to all of mankind.

To the woman He said, "I will greatly increase your pains in childbearing; with pain you will give birth to children…" (Genesis 3:16).

Instead of pain, the King James Version says "sorrow"—
etsab in Hebrew—meaning "usually (painful) toil; also a pang
(whether of body or mind)."[37]

Another meaning for *qayin*, or Cain, is "fixity, a lance (as
striking fast)."[38] In other words, Eve felt as if her stomach
was a painful boil, and Cain "lanced" it, relieving her pain
when he was born. When her pain finally stopped, Eve
named her son Cain, because he fixed her pain.

Now when a woman takes the attitude that her son is the
answer to her problem of an unloving or inattentive husband, she is in deep trouble—and so is the son! She will try to
make that son's love a substitute for the love of her absentee
husband. She will dote on that son, and teach him to dote on
her! She will gradually begin to *distort* her son's personality,
and he will begin to distort himself.

When he grows up, he often totally revolts against
women, becoming a homosexual. Or, if he marries, he will
naturally take that distortion into his own marriage, choosing someone like his mother, someone who will continue to
control things. Another alternative choice is that, all of his
life, he knows he has been controlled by his mother. So now
he thinks he has someone to control and all the resentment
of having his manhood warped will come out on his wife. He
will heap abuse on her with the tight grip of control. It will
be ugly, painful, and miserable for his wife.

When Eve declared, "I have gotten a man," according to
the original Hebrew, she was saying, "I have *erected* or *created*
a man."[39]

A possessive mother may think, "I made this guy. I pro-
duced him. I have purchased him. I paid a price. I lamented
for him. *I own him. He is my property; he belongs to me!*"

A possessive mother gets affirmation from her child. She holds him and loves him, and the boy naturally accepts and loves her. He affirms her, and she strokes him. Her son makes her feel wanted, needed, and important. Her husband makes her feel insignificant, but her son makes her feel significant. *This is not a healthy relationship.*

When Cain killed his own brother Abel, God said, "When you work the ground, it will no longer yield its crops for you. You will be a restless wanderer on the earth" (Gen. 4:12). The King James Version says he would be "a fugitive and a vagabond."

Like Cain, many men are wandering through their marriages and relationships as fugitives and vagabonds, neglecting their wives and children. Cain's sin was a direct result of his father's neglect toward his sons and his mother's overbearing control. We need to break the vicious cycle of neglect that threatens to destroy our children even in this generation. It makes them remorseless murderers full of jealousy, bitterness, and revenge. It is time to stand up, redeem, and protect our families!

Chapter 10

A Gentle and Quiet Spirit

*Wives, in the same way be **submissive** to your husbands so that, if any of them do not believe the word, they may be won over without words by the behavior of their wives, when they see the purity and reverence of your lives* (1 Peter 3:1-2).

One of the most despised and misunderstood words in the English language is the word *submission.*

Why would this word be so important to healthy marriages?

Who is supposed to do the "submitting" and to whom is that one to submit?

The answers may surprise you. Perhaps you were not surprised to see this Scripture passage at the top of this chapter with the "s" word, but do you really understand what the word means?

The Greek word translated as "submissive" (or "subjection" in the KJV) is *hupotasso.* The first part of the word, *hupo,* means "under." The second part, *tasso,* means "to arrange in an orderly manner."[40] So what Peter was saying is, "Wives, arrange yourselves in an orderly manner under your husband's covering."

Or, as I like to say it: "Wives, adjust yourselves to the circumstances under which your marriages must exist."

The majority of Christians in the first-century Church were females, as is the case today. Perhaps that is why Peter spent six verses dealing with born-again women whose husbands were unsaved and only one verse on the husband's role and attitude in marriage.

Women attend church more regularly and are more faithful in prayer, perhaps because, as we said earlier, they are worshipers by nature. Many husbands do not obey, believe, or even acknowledge the Bible. They don't go to church, and they don't even like for their wives to.

When these husbands see their wives exhibit reverence, chastity, and the fear of God, they will be won over to God. Before Smith Wigglesworth was saved, he was a British plumber who was so aggravated with his wife's devotion to church services that he literally locked her out of the house one night. He was won over to the Lord when she lovingly fixed him his breakfast after he opened the door the following morning to find her fast asleep on the porch.

I asked myself once why the apostle Peter wrote that women should seek "the unfading beauty of a gentle and quiet spirit, which is of great worth in God's sight" (1 Pet. 3:4b).

As I researched this verse, I discovered the Greek word translated "quiet" literally means "immovable" or "steadfast."[41] Peter was saying that, when you submit to authority, you should be gentle and quiet. A woman should "keep her seat, be still, be undisturbed, and be peaceable and silent, as in the sense of calmness."

After Wigglesworth received Christ, he began to win souls in the English tenement buildings where he was working on the plumbing. He entered full-time ministry in his 60's and made a lasting impression on the Church that continues to this day. It all began because a wife was submissive to her husband—even though he was against everything in which she believed. She knew her husband would never go to church to hear a sermon, so she lived a sermon in front of him in the home (see 1 Cor. 7:16).

A Tax on Your Prayers!

No, I am not cursing your prayers, but your actions toward your wife may be doing the job for you!

Peter warned husbands, "...in the same way be considerate as you live with your wives, and treat them with respect as the weaker partner and as heirs with you of the gracious gift of life, so that nothing will hinder your prayers" (1 Pet. 3:7).

Peter refers to wives as "the weaker partner" because they are more soft, delicate, or tender—not because they are less valuable. They simply need more protection. A good illustration of "weaker" in this context is that husbands are like heavy earthenware cups and saucers, while wives are like bone china. That kind of "dish" requires careful handling and cannot handle stress as well. It will usually chip, fracture, or break much easier than most other forms of pottery.

When a man does not treat his wife the way God intended, his prayers are "hindered," which means they are *delayed* or *sabotaged by the enemy*. We must honor our wives so that our ability to relate to God is not hindered. The word "hindered" in the Greek means "to excise or cut off."[42] In other words, if you do not treat your wife with honor, God will put an excise tax on your prayers. He will even cut them off, or at least cut them in half, and your needs will only be partially met.

If you fail to plant respect and consideration into your wife, then do not be surprised when your business, your ministry, and your dreams are frustrated. You did not plant or sow into your wife, so she could not incubate that seed. Your prayers will be frustrated or sabotaged because *your ability to relate to God* will be cut off or hedged in. What a sobering thought!

I have discovered in the 20 years we have been counseling troubled marriages through Higher Dimensions Ministries, that if the devil can sabotage the prayers of a husband, he can throw the whole family into disarray! God is showing me that my prayers cannot be properly handled in Heaven—nor even be regarded—if I do not work toward a healthy relationship with my wife, Gina.

That is because *men are seed planters*, but *women are seed incubators*. If I plant my seed of prayer, and my wife is not with me spiritually to incubate that seed (remember, we are "one" in the Lord), then my prayer is hindered from receiving a proper answer.

A man's seed can be planted in the earth, but if there is nothing to incubate that seed, nothing is germinated and nothing lives. I believe that principle applies to every area of our lives and relationships.

Marriage Changes Your Spiritual Life

When I was single, I felt complete on my own. My wife, Gina, felt the same way when she was single. But since I married (and God ordained this woman into my life and me into hers), I cannot be complete (maximized) without her.

I was complete before I married her, but now I am legally, spiritually, and scripturally interwoven into her life, and she into mine. I am no longer whole without my wife. She is not whole without me. The circumstances of "wholeness" change with marriage.

Another version of First Peter 3:7 tells men to live with their wives "understandingly." Most men do not live with their wives "according to knowledge" (KJV). We don't know who they are. We are not considerate of them because we don't understand them. We don't understand their laughter or their tears. So when they cry, we cut them off to suffer alone. When they laugh, we often think they are silly or "giddy or even okay."

We should be asking ourselves, "How can I understand this woman?"

Most men have heard all their lives, "You will never understand women, so don't even try."

If you buy into that old lie, you will never understand them and enjoy the kind of relationship in marriage God intended you to have. Men have blamed Eve down through the centuries for original sin because Adam blamed everything on "the woman whom Thou gavest to be with me" (Gen. 3:12 KJV). We have been putting the blame on women ever since. We do it both instinctively and habitually.

Adam may have been thinking at that point, "I did not ask for this woman. I was doing fine on my own, working in the garden, taking care of the trees and flowers, and walking and talking with You in the cool of the day. God, You were the One who said, 'It is not good for the man to be alone.' I was fine."

In other words, Adam was not about to take responsibility for Eve and how she had acted. Instead, he blamed God, saying, "After all, I did not ask for her. It is Your fault, God. She was *Your* idea, now she's *Your* problem. It was the way You created the human species and other mammals to be—male and female. I take no responsibility for it."

The main problem with today's deteriorating society is that everyone wants to disassociate him and herself from responsibility. We all want our "rights," but few want the accompanying responsibilities. Many are quick to say they came from dysfunctional families, but who didn't—including Adam and many of the Old Testament characters, not to mention Jesus and the early apostles. Everyone has some dysfunction in their background. That excuse will not "cut it" anymore.

It does not matter what your background is, you are responsible for your responses. You are "response-able," you have "response-abilities." God gave you the ability to respond appropriately to any circumstance or situation.

Of course, it is not always easy, but James 1:5 says, "If any of you lack wisdom, let him ask of God, who gives to all liberally and without reproach, and it will be given to him" (NKJ). Begin to accept the fact that you have certain responsibilities that you cannot negate or deny.

I interpret wisdom as "whys-dom." The "whys" of a thing helps determine and understand the "ways" of that thing. Once we ask God to show us why the woman (wife) exists, then we will better understand her ways. We must dwell with our wives according to knowledge, and knowledge comes from both experience and study. The more I study my wife, the more I understand and relate to God's methodology in her ways.

Responsibility Fosters Maturity

Webster's Dictionary defines "maturity" as "being full-grown, ripe, fully developed, perfect, complete, or ready."

Again, Dr. Cole says, "Maturity does not come with age; it begins instead with the acceptance of responsibility."

A man of 25 can be more mature than a man of 50, if he has consecrated himself to walk in the footsteps of Jesus and to listen with a will to learn. Jesus was only 33 when He was crucified, yet He was perfect in manhood, complete in His relationship with the Father, and ready to face the cross. To quote Dr. Cole again, "The difference between people who succeed and people who fail is their ability to handle adversity and pressure. Crisis is normal to life; it is the process by which we go from transient to permanent. Crisis doesn't make the person; it only exposes him for what he already is."

But solid food is for full-grown men, for those whose senses and mental faculties are trained by practice to discriminate and distinguish between what is morally good and noble and what is evil and contrary either to divine or human law. Therefore let us go on and get past the elementary stage...toward the completeness and perfection that belong to spiritual maturity... (Hebrews 5:14–6:1 AMP).

One characteristic of a mature man is that he is able to distinguish between good and evil. A responsible man recognizes the difference between right and wrong, and he thinks and acts rationally. He is accountable for his own behavior, rather than blaming his mistakes on others. He takes responsibility and assumes his obligations. He is dependable and reliable.

My son, give attention to my words; incline your ear to my sayings. Do not let them depart from your eyes; keep them in the midst of your heart; for they are life to those who find them, and health to all their flesh. Keep your heart with all diligence, for out of it spring the issues of life (Proverbs 4:20-23 NKJ).

We gain wisdom by reading the Word of God. Proverbs is filled with guidelines for living a successful life. But knowledge is a strange thing; it "leaks out of our heads." Unless we constantly remind ourselves of the truth, we forget. The Bible says, "So then faith cometh by hearing, and hearing by the word of God" (Rom. 10:17 KJV).

Do not let this Book of the Law depart from your mouth; meditate on it day and night, so that you may be careful to do everything written in it. Then you will be prosperous and successful (Joshua 1:8).

There is not a single issue of life, whether it concerns marriage, children, finances, health, or business, that is not covered by the Word of God. A spiritually mature man meditates on God's Word daily—that is, all day long, in and through every situation, decision, and circumstance.

I have noticed that mature Christian men are faithful to God, their families, their church, and their place of work. A real man keeps his word:

If he promises to help clean up the church grounds on Saturday, he shows up on time with a rake or a trash bag in hand.

If he promises to take his children fishing Saturday morning, you will find them at the lake that morning.

If he promises to take his wife to dinner or even to the mall on Friday night (now, hold steady, brothers), then he takes her to dinner (and not a fast-food place either). He also takes her to the mall, (even if he only waits for her in the car with the radio on). Yes, if it came out of his mouth, then you will find him practicing sacrificial love for his wife at the "Mall of Ever-growing Patience and Unlimited Credit Card Balances" (God help us all!).

God promotes faithfulness. He can promote a mature man into a position of authority because he can be trusted and counted on to keep his word. A faithful man is a blessed man who will prosper. He has to!

Blessed is the man who does not walk in the counsel of the wicked or stand in the way of sinners or sit in the seat of mockers. But his delight is in the law of the Lord, and on His law he meditates day and night. He is like a tree planted by streams of water, which yields its fruit in season and whose leaf does not wither. Whatever he does prospers (Psalm 1:1-3).

Dr. Cole has said, "It is possible to get spirituality from women, but strength always comes from men. A church, a family, a nation is only as strong as its men."

Adam was a brilliant man, but he was not a mature man. When the devil came slinking through the garden of Eden, Adam failed to recognize that the serpent was evil. He should have known better, because he is the one who named the serpent "hissing enchanter." He knew the seductive spirit, but was not mature enough to recognize its dangerous threat. He had known only good; so he was innocent to the wiles of satan, but not necessarily virtuous. Innocence is a condition a person is in before he knows the difference between right and wrong, good and evil. Virtue, on the other hand, is coming face to face with temptation and avoiding the evil for the good.

Some people have said, "Hey, that was not fair! If he was still young and untried, God should not have held him accountable!"

No, what happened *was* fair. Even a two-year-old can be held accountable for *obedience*. Adam knew he was supposed to obey God's one restriction, but he could have anything and everything else. He knew better. All Adam had to do was obey, but he chose to ignore God's warning. He was like a disobedient child.

Your beauty should not come from outward adornment, such as braided hair and the wearing of gold jewelry and fine clothes. Instead, it should be that of your inner self, the unfading beauty of a gentle and quiet spirit, which is of great worth in God's sight (1 Peter 3:3-4).

An immature man can't understand what goes on inside a woman, but *a mature man makes it his responsibility to understand*. He will help his wife become aware that her self-worth does not come from outward adornment—her hair, makeup, jewelry, or clothes—but rather from what is on the inside. There is nothing wrong with any of those things in moderation, but true beauty always shines outward from the heart. Peter did not denounce outward adornment. He was saying instead that, if a woman bases her identity and self-worth on those things, she has a problem.

Adam named Eve according to her function or position ("mother of all living things"), but he really did not know her or live with her "according to knowledge." He did not understand her unique physical and emotional structure. He did not understand that when a woman goes through cyclical hormonal changes in her body, her emotions change.

As a woman gives birth and nurses a baby, her body continually changes and responds to new demands with powerful hormonal surges that trigger dramatic physical— and emotional—changes. These powerful hormones affect all her biological systems. A man does not have those kind of changes going on in his body, so it is difficult for him to understand.

Because of this lack of understanding, many women are abused mercilessly during pregnancy by an immature and unlearned husband who does not know how to deal with his pregnant wife's unmanageable excitability.

The Greek word for "uterus" is *hystera*, from which we get the English words *hysteria, hysterical,* and *hysterectomy.* Many women are sent to shelters for abused women during their pregnancies. Why? It is because neither she nor her husband fully understand the dramatic and sometimes traumatic changes through which her body goes.

Remember, in Genesis 3:16, God said to Eve, "I will greatly increase your pains [and discomfort] in childbearing; with pain [aggravation and displeasure] you will give birth to children."

This again makes it absolutely mandatory that a man carefully study his wife in order to live with her "according to knowledge."

I Walk a Mile in Her Shoes

After studying my wife, Gina, I finally began to understand more about the delicacy, the tenderness, and the daintiness of the female nature in her. Each time I watch her nurture our son and observe the tender intimacy between them, I try to better understand their special relationship.

I finally had a breakthrough the day I changed places with Gina to become "Mr. Mom" of the Pearson household. Now I have a much more realistic understanding of what my wife goes through every day. The day I "walked a mile in my wife's shoes," Gina went upstairs to *my anointed desk* to use *my anointed study materials* to prepare a message she was scheduled to give.

Meanwhile, Pastor Carlton Pearson was downstairs holding the baby, changing diapers (how can one kid accomplish so much with so little?), cooking the food, and running back and forth. So far, so good. I even managed to steam out Gina's dress and hang it up for her.

Things started going downhill when I came into the bedroom with Julian while Gina was fixing her hair. Normally, my loving wife lets me make suggestions about her appearance, but not that day.

She politely but firmly said, "Honey, I have my mind on other things. Would you please leave while I fix my hair?"

So obediently, but reluctantly, I retreated with Julian and went back to the stew. After Gina left for her speaking engagement, I played with my son for the next four hours. I talked to him, fed him, and crawled around on the floor with him (that was when I remembered I had "40-something knees" compared to Julian's latest models).

Julian did not make a fuss about anything...not even his nap. He was perfect—until Gina walked back through the door. Naturally, he started crying the second he saw Mama.

Gina got that proud "Mama's gonna save you" look, the one that also says, "Oh, honey, what have you done to my poor little baby?"

Why is it that husbands cannot help feeling—and looking—guilty, when we have not done anything! But you see, mamas and their babies have a special bond. So once again I stepped aside, nursing my aching knees and trying to master my growing martyr's complex, while I watched the magic of the intimacy between the woman I love and the son for which I have always longed.

Only in recent years have men been allowed in a hospital's birthing suite. Before that, generations of men were pushed out of the picture and the process by legions of mothers, mothers-in-law, grandmothers, and midwives who supervised and dominated the birth process.

They kept the process shrouded in mystery, jealously guarding the door and closing the windows to make sure no "useless husband" blundered in to help. This left the anxious husband separated, secluded, and alone to listen helplessly to his wife's moans and/or screams of labor—while he paced in the living room at home, or in a sterile waiting room at a hospital.

Once the baby was home, he still did not know what to do (that part has not changed). Here again is a place where women in caring, but insensitive, error begin to build a wedge between the father and his children. If or when a father is kept away from his infant, or is made to feel "out of place" or overly awkward in holding or in any way attending to his child, he may begin to develop both a disdain and a dislike for participating in the early years of child rearing.

Mothers need to be especially careful about making their husbands feel welcomed and valued as companions and co-caretakers of the children. When babies are continually snatched from the father, or when the father is continually made to feel "stupid," unlearned, or unwelcomed where care of the baby is concerned, he will slowly but surely move aside. He may eventually completely retreat from a very important time and area of the child's initial upbringing and nurturing. Those precious and tender times can never by recovered.

Initially, when our son Julian was born, I thought Gina was overly protective and almost defensive about what he should eat, what lotions or soaps should be used, what brand of diapers or powders, and so forth, were used. She even asked me not to kiss him on the mouth in order not to expose him to adult germs.

That is when I put my foot down and said, "Enough is enough. You are beginning to shut me out of my son's existence, and I refuse to leave. I've waited for 40 years to have my own child, and nothing and nobody is going to stop me from kissing him anytime and anywhere I want to."

She then realized that even in her good intentions, she was violating my fatherly rights to my own child. We now have a much better understanding. Some women never learn that lesson, and the shut-out fathers never regain a closeness to their children.

It is not surprising that women feel possessive and have a proprietary attitude toward homemaking and child rearing. For centuries, that was the only area in which they had any authority whatsoever.

Women Were "Property" Until This Century

The culture of the Bible, especially the New Testament, revolves around the primitive cultures of the Romans, the Greeks, and the Jews. At that time, a woman was considered less than a second-class citizen by both ethical and moral standards. In all three cultures, she was more or less considered property a man would "own," just as he owned livestock. At best, she was looked upon and treated as a submissive and nearly ignorant, untrained, or inexperienced child.

Under Roman law, which prevailed everywhere Christians resided during the era of the New Testament, a woman had no rights. By law, she remained a child forever. When she lived in her father's house, she was under the *patria protestus*, which means the "father's power" in Latin. He literally had the power of life and death over her. When she married, she was transferred to be under the equally extreme power of her husband. She was completely subject to her husband and at his mercy. Actually, this also was true of British and American society until the early part of this century. Women had to be "emancipated" (the eighteenth amendment) just as slaves did, and emancipation from slavery came at least 75 years before women were given voting and property rights.

Roman women were prohibited from drinking wine. Cato, a typical ancient Roman and a senator, wrote, "If you were to capture [your] wife in an act of infidelity, you could kill her with impunity [meaning without punishment or trial]. But if she were to catch you, she would not venture to touch you with her finger. And indeed, she has no right" (end of quote)!

That was the prevailing thought in the Roman-Latin world. Under the Roman moral code, all the obligation was placed on the wife, and all the privilege was reserved for the husband. In the Jewish Talmud, a collection of commentaries, prayers, and stories concerning the Torah (the Jewish Bible, including the Pentateuch), one prayer the men prayed regularly was to thank God for not having been born a woman.

Christian or "Christ-like" ethics, however, never grant privilege without corresponding delegation. This was a revolutionary concept in those days. Suddenly, the woman had spiritual equality.

Like Peter, the apostle Paul devoted a significant part of his epistles to women, telling them how to deal with their spiritual equality. He knew the law said a woman was owned by her husband and was little more than his "property."

The introduction of the Christian concepts of freedom and personal value created a potentially explosive situation in the typical Roman, Greek, or Jewish home. When a woman in these cultures was saved, she would faithfully attend church and love and worship God—while her husband was at home thundering violent threats against her.

Each time Paul dealt with male and female relations, he began by telling women to submit. We need to remember that Paul was a Jew, and most men in the Church in his day came from a society that had been heavily influenced by the first-century cultural standards and attitudes.

Even today, many men still believe a woman is less than a man. If you travel to the Middle East, it is common to see a man riding a burro while his wife walks beside him. In India and Islamic countries, women still have no rights. In China, baby girls reportedly are still sometimes thrown onto trash heaps to die. Only one or two children are allowed to a couple, and they want at least one boy.

Even in this country, especially in Arab or Moslem circles, you may see a woman wrapped from head to toe in a dark muslin cloth with a veil, and carrying the baby. She will probably be accompanied by a man wearing a pair of Levis and a fashionable, open-necked shirt. Even American woman who marry into that culture are taught to be quiet and stay out of sight. They are to have no opinion.

A Mother's Power

In most of American society, the situation is totally opposite. Most men think women have too many opinions! Many men have an inherent disdain and hatred for women because they grew up depending on their mothers for everything, especially if she was a single parent.

Not only did they receive their meals from their mothers, but their mother was their main teacher and guide. Their mothers nursed them from the beginning years of life. Even without meaning to, boys feel suffocated by feminine authority.

A male human being is born with an inherent knowledge that he is to have authority and responsibility under God, just as every human, male and female, is born with a "God-shaped" space in their hearts that never can be filled satisfactorily with anything but God. Mothers need to know when to "let go and let grow." This becomes very difficult in a family with no father to take over as model and guide.

Teenage girls get into trouble because of seeking "father love" or simply someone to love them. They think babies will fill that void. Instead, a baby is a demanding little person, not capable of loving anyone. Meanwhile, boys move through the teen years flexing their "personality muscles," wavering between fear of this weight of headship they feel on their shoulders and "macho" feelings of being able to handle anything.

In some cases, the woman does not ever let go of the extreme authority from the early nurturing years, and seeds of hatred and resentment are planted in her son that may erupt violently in later years.

A mother has a natural hold on a man's life like no other.

Take, for instance, the biggest, meanest man you will ever find who has just robbed a convenience store. He is surrounded by SWAT teams and ten police vehicles with lights flashing. Nervous police officers have their Uzis pointed at him; police dogs are moved into position in hopes of keeping him from killing someone. Suddenly, the noisy mob pressing against the police barriers parts, and out walks a stooped-over old lady with a little hair net on her head, wearing support stockings and carrying a battered purse.

"Junior! Junior!" she shouts, as police and dogs turn to see who crossed the safety barrier so fearlessly. "Junior, what are you doing?"

She marches past the black-garbed SWAT team members, rises on her tiptoes, and grabs the 325-pound, 6-foot 5-inch felon by the ear, as he timidly whimpers, "Nothing, Mama. I'm coming."

The combined might and firepower of the penal system may not be able to handle him, but his mama knows what to say! God has put that kind of power into the hands of a mother. But *if a woman is not properly enhanced by her husband, she will abuse that power.* If you abuse your wife, she will abuse her power over your children, especially your sons.

In the first few months after our wedding, it was easy for me to give Gina things: clothes, jewelry, a new home, furniture, vacation trips, and so forth. However, after a while I was confronted with the difference between giving myself to her and giving up myself for her. There is a significant difference. One requires sacrifice; the other requires death to self. When we fail to understand a woman, we try to escape, either physically, emotionally, or spiritually. You cannot help your wife become all she is called to be in Christ until you are willing to *give up yourself* for her sake.

Let me share a secret with you: A woman will gladly submit to a man who is always concerned about her well-being. That kind of man is patient, kind, and loving. He will protect her and guard her with his life. Are you that kind of man?

Chapter 11

The Key to Blessings: Love, Honor, and Cherish

Husbands, love your wives, just as Christ loved the church and gave Himself up for her to make her holy, cleansing her by the washing with water through the word, and to present her to Himself as a radiant church, without stain or wrinkle or any other blemish, but holy and blameless (Ephesians 5:25-27).

One evening Gina and I were having an argument. She likes to pray every night before we go to sleep, but because I was upset—actually angry—I did not want to pray with her. I wanted to go upstairs and "pray to God by myself."

That night, she said, "Do you want to pray?"

I said, "No, but if you want to, you lead it."

"No, I would like for you to lead it," Gina said.

"I do not want to lead it," I replied. "You go ahead and pray, honey, and maybe I'll close it."

There was no way I was going to let her get the last word in with God! But then the thought occurred to me, *If I don't pray with my wife and understand her, if I don't plant seeds of prayer for her to incubate, God is not hearing my prayer anyway. I am sabotaging my own prayer life.*

"Sweetheart," I said, "I cannot be whole without you, and you cannot be whole without me." So I swallowed my pride and prayed.

I have prayed for thousands of people over the past 40 years. I have prayed that they would be saved and healed and that the Lord would continue to use my life for His glory, etc. But now that I am married, if I do not invest in my wife, it does not work the same way.

As we discussed earlier, according to the Scriptures, if I do not show consideration toward Gina, my prayers are hindered and sabotaged. My prayers become painful. I lament and mourn as though I were beating my breast in grief. It is as though my prayers bounce back off the ceiling.

The law of sowing and reaping applies to our marriage relationship as well as to finances. Our actions speak louder than words with the Lord and with our wives. When we honor our wives, we respect them. That means we value them, we esteem them, we dignify them, and we treat them as precious.

If you grew up in the typical American home hearing your father dismiss your mother's feelings, then your natural tendency will be to follow his sorry example. When you have a fight, all you have to do is accuse her of being in a "mood" and head for the door. Have you ever wondered why she follows you from room to room, saying, "We need to talk"? She does not want you to leave. She is actually begging you to stay.

If you are stuck in the traditional ignorance rut, then instead of considering your wife's needs, you will perfectly imitate what generations of men did before you.

You will slam out of the house with your car keys, mumbling to yourself, "I am not puttin' up with this stuff. I'm going to church. Don't I have a speaking engagement out of town somewhere, or can't I find one somewhere? Book my next meeting, God, because I'm outta here! Maybe she will repent and get right with You while I'm gone. Lord, she's in Your hands! Where's my road manager?"

You might as well stay home and resolve your differences. How can God bless you in ministry when you have that kind of resentment toward your wife?

In our anger and hurt, we do not hear what our wives are really saying: "Please don't leave me," they're pleading. "Hug me and tell me it is going to be all right. Affirm me. Don't leave me in the house all alone with this unmanageable monster inside me. I don't know what's going on inside my body, but God gave me to you. Help me. Stand with me. Hold me. Embrace me. Love me. Be a responsible man!" That is what every woman really wants from the man in her life. They need us; she needs you!

Don't Leave Her Hanging Off a Cliff

We are to treat our wives as joint heirs with us in Jesus—because they are! Pastor Brent Sharpe, the director of counseling at Higher Dimensions, has taught us this illustration to help us understand our relationship with our wives:

> "If you are climbing a mountain, and your partner is weaker, are you just going to leave him hanging? No, you reach out your hand and encourage him. 'Come on. You can make it.' That does not mean he is any less valuable to the team. He just has different strengths."

Frankly, most men are rougher on their wives than they are on male acquaintances who do not match their own strengths in team sports activities or business functions. They work with their friends' strengths, and cover or support them where they are weak. Once the men step into their own houses with their wives, however, they pull out critical attitudes and cutting words once again.

Adam knew Eve was different the moment he first saw her, but he did not know what was inside her. He did not know her true function or the gift she would bring to their existence. He called her "bone of my bones and flesh of my flesh...woman" (Gen. 2:23), and then he went back to work. It is all right, "Adam," to go back to work; but the time will come when you will have to connect with your wife more intimately and more definitively.

In some ways, things really have not changed since Adam's day in the garden. If you cut off your wife as Adam cut off Eve, then that guy with the snakeskin boots will start talking to her again. He will attend to her needs and minister to her, but you won't like what he is going to say. Satan knows that if he starts asking her questions and gives her the chance to express her feelings, he can seduce her and rob you both of the future.

You have one choice: Decide right now to *stop running away*, saying, "I cannot take it anymore. I do not need this. It is too hard. I am not made for a wife and kids."

Women are natural nesters. They can commit to a relationship. That is why the best workers are usually women. They are loyal and instinctively give of themselves wholly. They "commit" to other people more easily.

On the other hand, men are always tentative. They are built for the competition, battle, and continual sparring of the workplace, the financial arena, and the breadwinner's role. This includes a certain level of habitual suspicion and caution.

A man always thinks, "If this does not work, I can do thus and so."

He is always planning a way of escape, or a "Plan B." He rationalizes this by believing he is just "thinking ahead" when in actuallity he is thinking about how he can get rid of a woman if she suffocates him. Some men spend more time manipulating and scheming for ways to get out of responsibility than on focusing on how to fulfill their God-given duties within that responsibility.

A wife can either sap your energy or rejuvenate you. An old preacher used to tell us, "Brothers, a woman can either help you go to the lofty heights of ultimate success and happiness, or she could make you curse the very day you were born." Remember, the law of sowing and reaping applies to your relationship with your wife as well as with finances. If you release virtue into her, she will gladly receive it. When she gives it to you, you gladly receive it as well. Jesus said that when the woman with the issue of blood touched the hem of His garment, virtue went out of Him (see Mk. 5:30 KJV). He literally felt energy go out of Him. How did He replace that virtue or energy? He was renewed through His *intimacy* with the Father.

When someone steals your energy, and you do not have intimacy with the Father to replenish your strength, you will usually try to "fix your own problems" without His help. If you have not already discovered it the hard way, then let me warn you that you have *no power* in the flesh (except the power to fail). And most of us already have that down to a fine science.

We need to draw our strength and power from the Holy Spirit. We need to walk in intimate relationship with God. Then when someone saps us dry, we know how to be replenished by the Holy Ghost. If you are married, one of the most important ways God renews you is through your intimate relationship with your wife! (And I am not just talking about sex.)

It Is Good to Be Home!

I get the most wonderful feeling when I drive my car into the garage at the end of a long day, knowing Gina and Julian will be there to meet me. Gina always says, "Hi, Papa!" My son really gurgles at me at this point. Each time, I breathe a deep sigh of relief. Yes, *"it is so good to be home!"*

What kind of feeling would I get if I drove into the garage after a long day and Gina said, "Where have you been, Carlton Pearson? Did you get the bread? Why are you ten minutes late? Oh, never mind! The food's already on the table and getting cold—and don't bother asking me to heat if up for you. Get your own drink; I'm busy."

I don't know about you, but that would depress me. Christian wives have a responsibility to replenish their husbands. As usual, when we fail to follow God's plan and do it His way, we always pay.

I meet many preacher friends who say things like, "My wife will not work with me. I cannot seem to get anything going. I try this, and I try that, but I keep hitting roadblocks."

The enemy knows that. He has never forgotten what he heard in the garden centuries ago: "It is not good for the man to be alone." He knows that the marriage bond is meaningless unless the two partners bond. He will keep busting your brains out until you learn how to live "according to knowledge" with your wife so she can help you.

If you are mistreating your wife, or even if you are just "out of fellowship" with her, you will not be able to break through with your prayers. Your dreams, your visions, and the work of your hands will not prosper until you learn to nurture her; the two go hand in hand.

Look at the flip side of the marriage coin. When your wife is able to hook up with your vision and stand behind you 100 percent, there won't be anything you cannot accomplish! God will move Heaven and earth to answer your prayers. Brother, God demands obedience in this area. He has told us to love our wives as Christ loved the Church, and He cannot say it any plainer.

Jesus was willing to die to save us...the Church...His Bride. Are you willing to die for your wife?

Are you willing to give up football games, shooting hoops, or your golf game?

Are you willing to spend time with her, reading to her from the Word of God?

Are you willing to pray with her?

Which will you choose—blessings or cursings? It is up to you.

Chapter 12

Jesus: The Perfect Man

Till we all come in the unity of the faith, and of the knowledge of the Son of God, unto a perfect man, unto the measure of the stature of the fullness of Christ (Ephesians 4:13 KJV).

Do you remember all those paintings of Jesus you used to see when you were growing up?

You know...those lily-white, semi-effeminate pictures that used to hang on the walls of almost every Sunday school room in America? He always looked thin and powerless to me in those pictures. It is no wonder that a lot of men have rejected Him. To them, the "Jesus of the Sunday school room" looked as if He could not fight His way out of a wet paper sack, let alone fight their battles!

For who has known or understood the mind (the counsels and purposes) of the Lord so as to guide and instruct Him and give Him knowledge? But we have the mind of Christ (the Messiah) and do hold the thoughts (feelings and purposes) of His heart (1 Corinthians 2:16 AMP).

What we do not realize is that most of those paintings were done by Italian and Dutch artists who had never seen a

---

Jewish man bronzed by the Middle Eastern sun! They painted even scriptural themes in the style of their own time, fashions, hairstyles, and "religious" ideas. Erase those images of a malnourished, pale-looking, underdeveloped weakling. *Jesus was not a wimp!*

Even born-again men sometimes have a hard time identifying with their Savior because they think there is no way He (the emaciated man burned into their brains as "Jesus") could understand what a real-life man goes through. Let me bring you a "more perfect knowledge" of the *real man we call Jesus.*

Jesus the Carpenter

Is not this the Carpenter, the son of Mary and the brother of James and Joses and Judas and Simon? And are not His sisters here among us? And they took offense at Him and were hurt [that is, they disapproved of Him, and it hindered them from acknowledging His authority] and they were caused to stumble and fall (Mark 6:3 AMP).

A carpenter in those times was a craftsman or workman who built or repaired things in wood—primarily large structures for dwellings or purposes of commerce. Is it not interesting that Jesus was a man who could take a limb of a tree and make it into something useful—a chair, a table, a house, or a shop? Is that not what He is still doing with us...turning us into vessels fit for the Master's use, and tabernacles or houses for Him to dwell in?

The world today has trouble identifying with Jesus because they view Him as physically weak and powerless; however, the people in His own hometown of Nazareth had the opposite problem—they had a hard time seeing Him as anything more than a muscular, blue-collar worker.

Have you ever seen or felt a carpenter's hands? They are rough and calloused from swinging a hammer and handling wood. Craftsmen have broad shoulders and powerful arms. When they work outside in the summer, their skin turns dark mahogany.

Why would Jesus be any different? As a carpenter, He spent most of His time outdoors. He could not run down to the local lumber yard, buy His supplies, and have them delivered by truck to the building site. In those days, carpenters had to cut down their own trees, drag them down manually from the mountains, and then plane those raw tree trunks into usable planks and boards. They didn't have electric tools to help them, either. Their work was hard labor, done with crude tools that depended 100 percent on muscle power.

I believe Jesus' skin was probably a deep bronze. He would have had powerful muscles built through years of harvesting and preparing trees, and hoisting thick beams up to the tops of houses and other structures. No matter how you look at it: *Jesus was a man's man!*

Even after He gave up His father Joseph's business, He and His disciples *walked* from one end of Palestine to the other, up and over mountains and down through rocky valleys, preaching the gospel. Jesus was not too shabby at handling a fishing net either.

The wimpy Jesus I saw in pictures as a kid would not have entered the temple area to physically drive out the men who were buying and selling there. But a muscular Jesus overturned the money changers' heavy tables piled high with thousands of metal coins, and the benches of those selling doves.

"It is written," He said to them, *" 'My house will be called a house of prayer,' but you are making it a 'den of robbers' "* (Matthew 21:13).

Does that sound like a man who was weak and powerless? Aren't you glad He's on our side? Demons tremble at the very sound of His name, so why should we fear them? He is the Greater One living inside us.

Dr. Cole gives a powerful description of our Lord and Savior in his book *Maximized Manhood*:

"Jesus was a perfect balance of the tender and tough. He revealed His tenderness in His messages of love, His actions of healing and comforting, His death on the cross.

"But—the same Jesus who swept little children up into His arms gripped that scourge of cords and drove the money-changers out of the temple....

"Jesus was a fearless leader, defeating Satan, casting out demons, commanding nature, rebuking hypocrites. He had a nobility of character and a full complement of virtues which can be reproduced in us today—by the same Holy Spirit that dwelt in Him.

"God wants to reproduce this manhood in all men. What kind of manhood? Christlikeness! Christlikeness and manhood are synonymous."[43]

Jesus is a perfect example of godly manhood for every man among us. He had substance and maturity. He was not afraid to stand up for what He believed. He was fully God, yet He was fully man.

When I saw Him, I fell at His feet as though dead. Then He placed His right hand on me and said: "Do not be afraid. I am the First and the Last. I am the Living One; I was dead, and behold I am alive for ever and ever! And I hold the keys of death and Hades" (Revelation 1:17-18).

Jesus is the Alpha and the Omega, the Beginning and the End. The Man who threw out the money changers was pre-existent with the Father. He has always been and will always be, yet He was also the powerfully built Nazarene carpenter who knew how to frame a door and haul in a fishing net with equal skill. (By the way He could also cook up a seaside meal of fried fish with all the trimmings—see John 21:4-13.)

In the beginning was the Word, and the Word was with God, and the Word was God. He was with God in the beginning. Through Him all things were made; without Him nothing was made that has been made. In Him was life, and that life was the light of men (John 1:1-4).

Jesus is the Living Word. He is the second Person of the Holy Trinity. That kind of power is almost incomprehensible, is it not? Yet the Word of God says it is true. It also says that when you receive Jesus as your Lord and Savior, when you confess Him before men, that same God—Jesus—takes up residence inside you through His Holy Spirit.

We Are His Body and His Hands

I have strength for all things in Christ Who empowers me [I am ready for anything and equal to anything through Him Who infuses inner strength into me; I am self-sufficient in Christ's sufficiency] (Philippians 4:13 AMP).

What does it mean to be in Christ?

Webster's Dictionary defines the preposition *in* as "contained or enclosed by, inside, within, wearing, clothed by, and surrounded by." That means that when you are in Christ, you are *completely permeated* by the Son of God!

I have been crucified with Christ and I no longer live, but Christ lives in me. The life I live in the body, I live by faith in the Son of God, who loved me and gave Himself for me (Galatians 2:20).

We are literally the Body of Christ! Get that truth down into your spirit. Christ lives within us, and we are now the temple of the Holy Ghost.

Brother, look down at your hands. You may be a carpenter or a construction worker with the rough and calloused hands common to your trade. You may be a computer operator or programmer, or an accountant or doctor with hands that are soft and smooth. Your hands may be black or white, yellow or red, or even some color in between. They may be old and wrinkled, or young and yet unblemished by the marks of age, weather, and the scars of life.

Whether your hands are crippled or strong, they are Christ's hands, if you are a born-again believer. As you read the words on this page, they are the only hands He has to accomplish His work on this earth. *Jesus works through people*, and until you understand who you are in Christ, you will have no power to serve Him.

It is like having a power saw stored in the garage. If you do not know how to turn the power switch on, you will keep sawing wood the old-fashioned way—through your own strength. Or it is like having a Cadillac or Porsche in the garage while still walking to the bus stop each day—because you do not know how to turn the key on!

God Has a Plan for You

For we are God's workmanship, created in Christ Jesus to do good works, which God prepared in advance for us to do (Ephesians 2:10).

You were created for a purpose. But make no mistake: The devil will do anything he can to keep you from fulfilling God's plan for your life! However, he cannot do that if you open your eyes and look to the Author and Finisher of your faith (see Heb. 12:2).

In Jeremiah 1:5 God says, "Before I formed you in the womb I knew you...." God knows your name, just like He knows my name. He knows your heart and your wife's heart, if you're married, just like He knows my heart. He knows your purpose, and He longs to see you fulfill it.

You may have lived every day until this moment thinking, "I am just a nobody. I was born a nobody and I'll die a nobody."

The devil has lied to you! He has whispered wicked enchantments into your mind to convince you that you are "not good enough" or "not clever enough or smart enough" to walk in victory. I am telling you right now that you have been listening to a lie straight out of the pit of hell! You think you cannot repent, or change, or do anything differently than you do it now. It is just not true.

You think you cannot talk to your wife. The snake has convinced you there is no way you can stop yelling at her or treating her like a second-class citizen. I am here to tell you that you can! *Who told you that you were naked?* The devil did...and he is the same liar who tricked Adam and Eve. For-get his empty hissing and start listening to what the Almighty God says about you in the Bible:

You are the salt of the earth... (Matthew 5:13).

You are the light of the world... (Matthew 5:14).

But as many as received Him, to them He gave the right to become children of God... (John 1:12 NKJ).

But I have called you friends.... You did not choose Me, but I chose you and appointed you that you should go and bear fruit, and that your fruit should remain... (John 15:15b-16 NKJ).

And having been set free from sin, you became slaves of righteousness (Romans 6:18 NKJ).

For as many as are led by the Spirit of God, these are the sons of God (Romans 8:14 NKJ).

The Spirit Himself bears witness with our spirit that we are children of God, and if children, then heirs—heirs of God and joint heirs with Christ... (Romans 8:16-17 NKJ).

For He made Him who knew no sin to be sin for us, that we might become the righteousness of God in Him (2 Corin-thians 5:21 NKJ).

Therefore you are no longer a slave but a son, and if a son, then an heir of God through Christ (Galatians 4:7 NKJ).

But now in Christ Jesus you who once were far off have been brought near by the blood of Christ (Ephesians 2:13 NKJ).

For our citizenship is in heaven... (Philippians 3:20 NKJ).

Set your mind on things above, not on things on the earth. For you died, and your life is hidden with Christ in God (Colossians 3:2-3 NKJ).

You are all sons of light and sons of the day (1 Thessalonians 5:5a NKJ).

Coming to Him as to a living stone, rejected indeed by men, but chosen by God and precious, you also, as living stones, are being built up a spiritual house, a holy priesthood, to offer up spiritual sacrifices acceptable to God through Jesus Christ (1 Peter 2:4-5 NKJ).

We know that whoever is born of God does not sin; but he who has been born of God keeps himself, and the wicked one does not touch him (1 John 5:18 NKJ).

The next time the devil tells you, "You are nothing," tell him he is a liar and the father of lies. Quote him some of these Scriptures. That is what Jesus did in the wilderness when He was tempted by satan.

Say, "It is written...I am the righteousness of God in Christ!"

You have the victory! Walk in it. Be a man and stand in the gap! God needs your hands.

Chapter 13

The Final Shaking

*At that time His voice shook the earth, but now He has prom-
ised, "Once more I will shake not only the earth but also the
heavens." The words "once more" indicate the removing of
what can be shaken–that is, created things–so that what
cannot be shaken may remain* (Hebrews 12:26-27).

The differences between men and women are profound
in their implications for building and maintaining community and culture in the human race.

Men seem lost and even "unneeded" according to some.
In contrast, the woman's social responsibility is obviously
tied to her sexual physiology, specifically her ability to con-
ceive, develop, bear, and nurse a child. Her entire biological
and psychological makeup are involved in this miracle, yet
the baby's growth is concealed and personal from all but the
eyes of the Creator.

The social implications of a woman's role in bearing children are great. The continuance of the human race, as well
as the whole economy, is based on the number of children
born each year and on their healthy growth. The birth rate
literally determines how many houses, how much food and

clothing, how many schools, and how many workers will be employed for the next two decades! Also, the successful defense of our nation rests on the number and quality of men available for military service.

The mother predominantly controls the psychological development of the child in its early years. We now know the influences of those years are important in determining a child's disposition and sense of security. Thus a mother's influence affects our society far beyond her lifetime.

The woman has an obvious claim to a parental relationship to a child. She carries, develops, and bears the child and nurses it for several months. Everyone from close friends and relatives to casual shoppers in a crowded mall can see the visible proof of her maternity during the nine-month gestation of her offspring. Doctors, nurses, and midwives can provide unquestionable witness to a mother's physical act of giving birth to her baby.

Where is the daddy in this picture?

I grew up in an area where a popular saying was, "Mama's baby, Daddy's maybe." What a sad commentary on modern life. The husband has an equal right to parenthood. His seed initiates the baby's development, contributes half of its genes, and determines the child's blood type; nevertheless, *his relationship is publicly unprovable* (except for very expensive and generally unavailable DNA-based paternity tests).

A man is not directly involved with the child during its long process of development and growth in the womb. He can go along for the prenatal checkups. He can stroke his wife's stomach, and sing to the baby in her womb in hopes that the child within will recognize his voice after birth. But the truth is that he can claim fatherhood only by the designation of the mother. In a society of lifelong monogamy, this is done by the marriage commitment. The father's claim is publicly accepted in the marriage ceremony. Nevertheless, the mother's power to grant the right of paternity is supreme and exclusive.

A Man's World Needs Women

The late psychologist, Dr. Margaret Mead, wrote, "Virtually nothing...in the whole set of male activities is equivalent to the finality of having a baby."[44]

As Gilder puts it, "In child bearing, every woman is capable of a feat of creativity and durable accomplishment, permanently and uniquely changing the face of the earth, that only the most extraordinary man can even pretend to duplicate in external activity."[45]

Men can create and build magnificent architecture and design cities. We can run governments and even be elected presidents and coronated as kings, but only a woman can produce another human being! She generally produces only one egg per month, while her mate will dispatch between 200 and 300 million microscopic sperm to chase that one egg.

The man seems to "give" so much more, yet it does not matter how much a man "has to give," if there is not a woman involved with her single egg, then all that masculine virility and fertility is of no consequence at all! As the old James Brown song says, it may be a "man's world," but it would be nothing without a woman or girl!

There is a mystical or spiritual side of marriage that can only be perceived by personal experience and revelation. My perceptions of women and of the role of the sexes have changed dramatically since I first preached about the things we have discussed in this book. What happened to bring such a big change in my thinking? Two world-changing events did it, and I am glad to say I will never be the same: *I married Gina, and then little Julian was born.* My whole understanding of the world took on a new perspective.

All of a sudden, I also had a new understanding of the significance of Jesus' first public miracle at the wedding at Cana. In the time of Jesus' earthly life, marriages were arranged and governed by Jewish custom. They were essentially joyless affairs, in spite of the spirited celebrations, because a woman in that culture had no worth. She had little or no input about whom she would marry.

It is significant that Jesus chose to turn water (a symbol of the Holy Spirit) into wine (a symbol of joy) at a marriage feast. In other words, His first miracle was to bring joy into a marriage and into people's lives! Jesus still brings true celebration to marriages where He is an invited guest!

Jesus valued women. In fact, His attitude about women got Him in trouble. He treated women as of equal value with men. If you search the Gospels, you will see that women supported His ministry. He treated them as persons of value. Even the apostle Paul's writings, which so many old-line fundamentalists and Pentecostalists used (and still use) to "keep women in their place," were revolutionary. In reality, Paul was not putting women down, but raising them up to equal consideration with men.

No Jewish rabbis had ever admonished men to love their wives, treat them fairly, and act as we now expect a good husband to act. Most of the rabbinical writings about women and marriage are such that even Christian women today who are not feminists would raise their eyebrows in horror.

Should we not follow in the footsteps of Jesus in this area as well as in all others? Should we not begin to value women in the same way? Women respond to a gentle touch motivated by genuine love and respect. Remember that the next time you are cold and distant with your wife.

Remember, one of the best ways to soothe a woman is by washing her. When your wife gets uptight, run her some bath water, add a few bath beads, and light a few candles. Play some soft music for her. I will guarantee that when she comes out of the bathroom, she will be a totally different person.

Set Aside Your Anger

Brother, it is time to stop penalizing your wife for her God-given emotions. She is the "womb-man"—the one who carries your children and nurtures them. Stop being angry because you need women in your life. God made you that way! I do not care how self-sufficient we like to think we are as men and leaders, we need our moms and our sisters, and above all, we need our wives!

Stop holding a grudge against them and trying to lord it over them because they were so long in control of you. Stop fighting for identity. Your identity is in Christ. Accept women for who they are.

If you have not matured to the point where you can control your anger, and you have to leave to keep from committing an act of violence against her, then leave the house for a while! But do not run off just because you are irresponsible—stand up and "face the music" like a man. You entered the marriage relationship for life; now is the time to back up your words of commitment with determination, patience, and love.

When men rise up and act like men, they have a certain gait in their walk. Brother, there ought to be a look of intelligent effervescence and sparkle in your eyes! You are a joint heir with Jesus, not some weak, beaten down, limp coward, slithering along at ground level like a snake. God told us to rule, subdue, and dominate this earth!

If you are a man, then it is your job to crush the devil's head. Let's start stomping on him! Let's stomp him out of our marriages! Let's stomp him out of our children! Let's stomp him out of our community, and yes, let's stomp him out of our churches too! Let's get busy with the duty of true manhood—to crush the head of the devil!

Maximize Your Victory!

Most races are won on the "second wind," when a runner's body responds to the command of the runner's drive to win. Get your second wind by praying in the Holy Ghost! The race is not given to the swift. The battle is not given to the strong. The victory is given to the one who *endures to the end*! Maximize yourself.

It is a sin for a man to become less than God has ordained him to be. Find out who you are and seek God's direction for your life. Set goals for success, not failure or mediocrity. The devil will tell you it is arrogance, but it is nothing more than God-inspired confidence.

Is there a man in your house?

Is there a real man who will run the devil out of town?

Is there a man in the house who will cast the devil out of our minds and out of the garden we call home?

We must close up the breach and bridge the gap as men of God. We must rise up in our most holy faith, full of the Holy Ghost! Today, I know there are mighty men of valor who have been raised up for such as time as this! There are mighty men filled with the Holy Ghost who need to step forward. The time has come for men to rise up!

Beware the incantations of the snake: *Culture should never take precedence over the convictions of the Word of God!* When the Holy Spirit is moving, He transcends cultural barriers. Racial and ethnic origins have nothing to do with it.

When the divine move of the Holy Spirit hits this planet again, it will go everywhere and include everyone...even Jews, Arabs, Hindus, Buddhists, and Moslems. The Chinese will speak in tongues en masse as a Holy Ghost wave sweeps over that continent. God is going to universalize the movement of the Spirit, and it is going to happen by the end of this decade. We need to be real men who refuse to let color, culture, or credentials separate us as we did at Azusa nearly a century ago! We need to be vessels fit for the Master's use! We need to get ready!

A New Millennium

We are only a few years away from our six thousandth anniversary as human beings. The new millennium actually begins on the first day of 2001. The year 2000 is the last year of the old decade, century, and millennium. According to biblical chronology, mankind is now 5,996 years old. Six is the number of man because on the sixth day, God created man. Six is one number less than seven, the number of perfection. On the seventh day, God's creation was complete and He rested.

This is not only the last decade in a century, it is also *the last decade in a millennium!* Some very unusual events are going to take place that have never been seen before. All of creation is groaning, waiting for the manifestation of the sons of God (see Rom. 8:22), the return of Jesus, and the reign of His Kingdom.

We need to be prepared to see an increase in social and political revolutions and natural disasters—we will see an unprecedented number of volcanic eruptions, earthquakes, floods, famines, and plagues. There will even be an increase in animal and insect attacks as lawlessness extends to the animal kingdom.

In the midst of all this darkness, the Church will rise out of the dust as fully manifested sons of God. It will be a glorious day! We will be the sons of God—the legacy-bearers, the name-bearers, the seed-bearers of God!

The prophet Isaiah declared, "For unto us a child is born, unto us a son is given" (Is. 9:6a KJV).

The spirit of sonship is coming again. If there was ever a time to get right with God and to imitate His nature, it is now. *The final shaking is about to take place.*

One year from now, in 1997, there will be dramatic changes in the world, not only politically and socially, but in the Church as well. I believe there will be *a conspicuous changing of the guard*—a change in leadership. Some very prominent leaders will be gathered home by the Lord in the next year—leaders you would not expect to go so soon.

The Holy Spirit has shown me that every minister who has been living on "synthetic faith" will be disqualified. Their ministries may be large, but if they did not build those ministries God's way—if God did not build the house—then God will stop them and tear down their house to lay a new foundation of holiness.

There are countless ministries today that are being propped up by mechanical life-support systems. They are "brain dead"; their "hearts" stopped responding to God years ago; their "kidneys" have failed; and their "lungs" have collapsed. I believe God Himself is going to pull the plug. Madison Avenue marketing tactics will no longer work—God is only interested in the "street called Straight."

God is going to demand that any ministry desiring to stand during the final shaking *be built on the raw power of the Holy Ghost*. It is coming! I believe whole denominations built on man's foundations will be shaken.

The Bible says that in the last days, men's hearts would fail them because of fear (see Lk. 21:26 KJV). I believe some congregations will see their ministers' hearts explode in their chests because they have been in rebellion against God. It will not just be "senior statesmen" in the Church who will be taken. Some young ministers will be taken in the prime of their lives.

As Christian men with a mandate to lead, we need to stand up and boldly declare to our collapsing world: "We are here to accomplish our mission, and when that mission is accomplished, we'll head on home."

These are critical and pivotal times in the history of the Church.

Get ready, brother—Jesus is coming soon! You need to get into the Word of God and "study to shew thyself approved" (2 Tim. 2:15 KJV).

It is time to *grow up* in the things of God. Now is the time to obey—the Church needs another man in the line of leadership. You need to become a mature leader that God can call and trust in these perilous times. Get serious and consecrate yourself to His purpose for your life! No one can do it for you.

God is counting on you. He gave you life because He has a place and a people that need your life. He needs mature men, responsible men, faithful men. He needs men who reflect the character of Jesus...strong men who are not afraid to stand up for what is right.

Is there a man in your house who will stand in the gap?

Is there a man in the house?

Are you that man?

Endnotes

1. Dr. Carl Wilson, Worldwide Discipleship Foundation.

2. James Strong, *The Comprehensive Concordance to the Bible*, (Iowa Falls, IA: World Bible Publishers, n.d.), *head* (#2776). (These meanings also come from their prime root words and so may not be exact to *Strong's*.)

3. *Strong's, bruise* (#7779).

4. *Strong's, alone* (#905).

5. *Strong's, man* (#120).

6. *Strong's, man* (#376).

7. *Strong's, man* (#45, 2145).

8. *Strong's, man* (#582, 605).

9. *Strong's, female* (#5347, 5344).

10. *Strong's, womb* (#7358, 7355, 7356).

11. *Strong's, Eve* (#32, 31, 2098).

12. *Strong's, helpmeet* (#5828, 5826).

13. *Strong's, dress* (#5647).

14. *Strong's, keep* (#8104).

15. Dr. Donald Joy, in an interview with Dr. James Dobson. "The Differences Between Male and Female," cassette #C8099, from Focus on the Family.

16. Dr. Joy, "The Differences Between Male and Female."

17. Anne Moir and David Jessel, *Brain Sex* (New York, NY: Bantam Doubleday Dell Publishing Group, Inc., 1992).

18. Gary Smalley, "Hidden Keys to Loving Relationships," tape series from Relationships Today, Inc. (1988).

19. Smalley, "Hidden Keys."

20. Smalley, "Hidden Keys."

21. Smalley, "Hidden Keys."

22. Smalley, "Hidden Keys."

23. Smalley, "Hidden Keys."

24. *Strong's, agreed* (#3259).

25. *Merriam Webster's Collegiate Dictionary*, 10th Ed. (Springfield, MA: Merriam-Webster, Inc., 1994).

26. *Strong's, serpent* (#5175, 5172).

27. *Strong's, serpent*, "vision, or to look at" (#3789, 3700).

28. Gordan Dalby, *Healing of the Masculine Soul* (Waco, TX: Word Books, 1988).

29. Dr. Carl W. Wilson, *Our Dance Has Turned to Death* (Wheaton, IL: Tyndale House Publishing, 1981).

30. Sara McLanahan & Gary Sandefur, *Growing Up With a Single Parent* (Cambridge, MA: Harvard University Press, 1994).

31. Dr. Edwin Louis Cole, *Maximized Manhood* (Tulsa, OK: Harrison House, 1985).

32. *Strong's, curse* (#2764).

33. Barbara Reynolds, commentary, *USA Today*.

34. Reynolds, *USA Today*.

35. Reynolds, *USA Today*.

36. *Strong's, Cain* (#7014, 7013, 7069, 6969).

37. *Strong's, pain, sorrow* (#6093, 6089).

38. *Strong's, Cain* (#7013).

39. *Strong's, gotten* (#7069).

40. *Strong's, submissive/subjection* (KJV) (#5293, 5259, 5021).

41. *Strong's, quiet* (#2272, 1476).

42. *Strong's, hindered* (#1581, 1537, 2875).

43. Dr. Cole, *Maximized Manhood*.

44. Dr. Margaret Mead, *One Aspect of Male and Female* (New York, NY: Fawcett, 1956).

45. Dr. George Gilder, *Sexual Suicide* (New York, NY: Bantam Books, 1975).

Carlton Pearson

The Man, The Ministry, The Message

One of the most dynamic and anointed preachers of our time, Evangelist Carlton Pearson shares the gospel with an electrifying presentation, communicates with unmistakable clarity, and challenges believers to return to holiness. He presents uncompromising truths with a unique style of humor that reaches far into the hearts of his listeners from coast to coast, young and old, and all ethnic origins.

Leaving San Diego to follow the burning desire in his heart to preach, Carlton attended Oral Roberts University in Tulsa, Oklahoma. Chosen as an ORU "World Action Singer," Carlton began to receive widespread exposure as he traveled with President Roberts across the nation and other parts of the world. Carlton's fresh and anointed approach to music and worship complemented Brother Roberts' faith-filled messages of healing and deliverance.

Following his student days at ORU, he became an Associate Evangelist for the Oral Roberts Evangelistic Association for nearly two years. In 1977 Carlton founded Higher Dimensions, which has evolved from a traveling evangelistic team to a multi-faceted ministry that includes a large local church in Tulsa, a crisis pregnancy center, a home for unwed mothers, an adoption agency, and a local and direct mail marketing facility for the distribution of service tapes, music cassettes, and Carlton's books.

The congregation of Higher Dimensions is composed of many ages, races, and cultures. One newspaper called it "a sociologist's fantasy, a compilation of people from every socio-economic class...a racial melting pot." Pastor Pearson prefers to call it "a stew." In a stew, each ingredient stays as it is, but together they begin to take on the "flavor" of one another. He places a high priority on family and country, reflected in his first television special, entitled: "America, We Love You."

Crusades here in America and abroad, as well as a rapidly growing national television ministry, have provided Carlton Pearson the opportunity to impact the lives of countless thousands and influence the works of other Christians as well.

Carlton Pearson serves on the board of regents at ORU, as well as on the boards of several Christian missionary organizations. He is also founder and president of the Azusa Interdenominational Fellowship of Christian Churches and Ministries, Inc., and initiated the great annual Azusa conferences held in Tulsa, Oklahoma, and takes the "Spirit of Azusa" to various cities nationwide as well.

He has authored a variety of books and booklets carrying the message of deliverance: that Jesus Christ came to forgive the sins of all men and save their souls.

In 1993 Carlton Pearson married the former Gina Gauthier. They are the proud parents of one son, Julian.

Destiny Image
New Releases

ANOINTED OR ANNOYING?
by Ken Gott.
Don't miss out on the powerful move of God that is in the earth today! When you encounter God's Presence in revival, you have a choice—accept it or reject it; become anointed or annoying! Ken Gott, former pastor of Sunderland Christian Centre and now head of Revival Now! International Ministries, calls you to examine your own heart and motives for pursuing God's anointing, and challenges you to walk a life of obedience!
ISBN 0-7684-1003-7 $9.99p

CROSS-POLLINATION
by Lila Terhune
Do you dream of a worldwide harvest of souls? Do you want to see God's manifest Presence here in the earth? Lila Terhune, lead intercessor for the Brownsville Revival, shares how to "cross-pollinate" the world with the glory of God. Join with intercessors from every nation who are preparing the way and opening the heavens for the next move of God!
ISBN 0-7684-1004-5 $10.99p

GOD CAN USE LITTLE OLE ME
by Randy Clark.
Do you believe that God uses only the educated, the dynamic, and the strong in faith to do the work of His Kingdom? Be prepared to be surprised! In this practical, down-to-earth book, Randy Clark shows that God uses ordinary people, often in extraordinary ways, to accomplish His purposes. Through his own personal experience and the testimonies of other "little ole me's," Randy shows that God still heals today, and that He is using everyday Christians to be involved with Him in a healing ministry to the world.
ISBN 1-56043-696-4 $9.99p

CORPORATE ANOINTING
by Kelley Varner.
Just as a united front is more powerful in battle, so is the anointing when Christians come together in unity! In this classic book, senior pastor Kelley Varner of Praise Tabernacle in Richlands, North Carolina, presents a powerful teaching and revelation that will change your life! Learn how God longs to reveal the fullness of Christ in the fullness of His Body in power and glory.
ISBN 0-7684-2011-3 $9.99p

Available at your local Christian bookstore.

Internet: http://www.reapernet.com

4:39

Other *Destiny Image titles* you will enjoy reading

THE BATTLE FOR THE SEED

by Dr. Patricia Morgan.

The dilemma facing young people today is a major concern for all parents. This important book shows God's way to change the condition of the young and advance God's purpose for every nation into the new century.

ISBN 1-56043-099-0 $9.99p

THE FATHERLESS GENERATION

by Doug Stringer.

With this book Doug Stringer will stir your heart and enflame your desire to reach this generation—and thus the nation—with an invitation to return to *the* Father! *The Fatherless Generation* presents the depth of the need and the hope of the solution—a relationship with Almighty God, our Father.

ISBN 1-56043-139-3 $8.99p

HOW TO RAISE CHILDREN OF DESTINY

by Dr. Patricia Morgan.

This groundbreaking book highlights the intricate link between the rise of young prophets, priests, and kings in the Body of Christ as national leaders and deliverers, and the salvation of a generation.

ISBN 1-56043-134-2 $9.99p

Available at your local Christian bookstore.

Internet: http://www.reapernet.com

4:40

Other *Destiny Image titles* you will enjoy reading

POT LIQUOR
by Dr. Millicent Thompson.

Did you know that you can learn more about life over a "bowl of collard greens and some good conversation" than you can learn on a therapist's couch? Hidden in shared stories and passed-down advice are life lessons that you can learn from without experiencing the pain. Like a full course spiritual meal, *Pot Liquor* is guaranteed to feed your soul and keep you coming back for more!
ISBN 1-56043-301-9 $9.99p

CRASHING SATAN'S PARTY
by Dr. Millicent Thompson.

Don't let satan hinder the power of God from working in your life any longer! In this book you'll discover the strategies and devices the enemy uses against you. Too many of us attribute our troubles to God when they are really of the devil. The adversary is subtle and delights in deception. We must be able to recognize *who* is doing *what* in our lives so that we can react according to God's Word. Learn how to destroy the works of the enemy. You can crash satan's party and overcome!
ISBN 1-56043-268-3 $10.99p

I STOOD IN THE FLAMES
by Dr. Wanda Davis-Turner.

If you have ever come to a point of depression, fear, or defeat, then you need this book! With honesty, truth, and clarity, Dr. Davis-Turner shares her hard-won principles for victory in the midst of the fire. You can turn satan's attack into a platform of strength and laughter!
ISBN 1-56043-275-6 $8.99p

SEX TRAPS
by Dr. Wanda Davis-Turner.

Discover the tactics of the enemy that lead you down the road of unparalleled remorse. Satan's traps are set with a burning desire to birth pain, guilt, and shame in your life. Learn to avoid the traps!
ISBN 1-56043-193-8 $8.99p
Also available as a workbook.
ISBN 1-56043-300-0 $7.99p

Available at your local Christian bookstore.

Internet: http://www.reapernet.com

Exciting titles
by Myles Munroe

UNDERSTANDING YOUR POTENTIAL

This is a motivating, provocative look at the awesome potential trapped within you, waiting to be realized. This book will cause you to be uncomfortable with your present state of accomplishment and dissatisfied with resting on your past success.
ISBN 1-56043-046-X $9.99p

RELEASING YOUR POTENTIAL

Here is a complete, integrated, principles-centered approach to releasing the awesome potential trapped within you. If you are frustrated by your dreams, ideas, and visions, this book will show you a step-by-step pathway to releasing your potential and igniting the wheels of purpose and productivity.
ISBN 1-56043-072-9 $9.99p

MAXIMIZING YOUR POTENTIAL

Are you bored with your latest success? Maybe you're frustrated at the prospect of retirement. This book will refire your passion for living! Learn to maximize the God-given potential lying dormant inside you through the practical, integrated, and penetrating concepts shared in this book. Go for the max—die empty!
ISBN 1-56043-105-9 $9.99p

IN PURSUIT OF PURPOSE

Best-selling author Myles Munroe reveals here the key to personal fulfillment: purpose. We must pursue purpose because our fulfillment in life depends upon our becoming what we were born to be and do. *In Pursuit of Purpose* will guide you on that path to finding purpose.
ISBN 1-56043-103-2 $9.99p

Available at your local Christian bookstore.

Internet: http://www.reapernet.com

4:42